The Ultimate U.S. Presidents Quiz

B.R. Egginton

<u>Contents</u>

Preface

'The freedom of Speech may be taken away – and, dumb and silent we may be led, like sheep, to the Slaughter.'
George Washington, 1783

'We won the Evangelicals, we won with young, we won with old, we won with highly educated, we won with poorly educated! I love the poorly educated.'
Donald Trump, 2016

Prepare yourself to embark on an epic journey through the history of the world's first nuclear power, the home of Hollywood, and innovator of big brands such as *Coca-Cola* and *Microsoft*.

In the ensuing pages are well over 1,000 questions, covering every president from George Washington to Donald Trump, as well as an abundance of issues: their personal lives, government legislation, and notable events of the times in which they served.

And with three levels of difficulty (easy, average and expert), there's something to suit everyone.

By the end of this journey of self-improvement, who knows who your favourite president will be? Will it be the usual suspects: George Washington, Franklin Roosevelt, et al? Or will you find yourself venturing off the beaten track; voicing support for one of the USA's unsung heroes?

There isn't a right or wrong answer. Greatness, after all, is not a fixed state: it changes based upon one's own personal interpretations and values.

Questions

George Washington 1 (easy)

Q1 What was George Washington's political affiliation when he served as President?

    A Republican
    B Democrat
    C Libertarian
    D Independent

Q2 Who served as George Washington's Vice President?

    A John Adams
    B Benjamin Franklin
    C Thomas Jefferson
    D Patrick Henry

Q3 What was the name of George Washington's wife?

    A Anna
    B Martha
    C Elsie
    D Hayley

Q4 What relation was John Parke Custis to George Washington?

    A Uncle
    B Grandfather
    C Stepson
    D Second cousin

Q5 How many terms did George Washington serve as President?

    A 1
    B 2
    C 3
    D 4

Q6 George Washington was a member of what church?

   A Catholic
   B Anglican
   C Presbyterian
   D Orthodox

Q7 How many children did George Washington have?

   A 0
   B 3
   C 5
   D 17

Q8 What did Valley Forge serve as?

   A Presidential palace
   B Military encampment
   C Prison
   D Port

Q9 As President, George Washington preferred to be referred to by what term of address?

   A Mr President
   B His Excellency
   C His Highness the President
   D Commander

Q10 George Washington was fiercely opposed to the formation of what?

   A Universities
   B Secret societies
   C Political parties
   D State militias

George Washington 2 (average)

Q1 What was the name of George Washington's plantation?

Q2 In what British colony was George Washington born?

Q3 George Washington was commander-in-chief of what army during the American Revolutionary War?

Q4 What percentage of the vote did George Washington receive to become President in 1789?

Q5 Thomas Hickey was executed for mutiny and sedition in 1776. But he was also accused of being involved in what plot?

Q6 Where was George Washington sworn in as the first President of the USA?

Q7 Which country defeated George Washington at the Battle of Fort Necessity?

Q8 'Victory or Death' was the code name of an operation where George Washington crossed what river?

Q9 What was the Panic of 1792?

Q10 What was the only place George Washington ever visited off the North American mainland?

George Washington 3 (expert)

Q1 In what year was George Washington's Farewell Address published?

Q2 What were the names of George Washington's parents?

Q3 At what farm did George Washington spend much of his childhood?

Q4 In what year was the State of Washington admitted to the Union?

Q5 An attempt was made to steal what from Mount Vernon in 1830?

Q6 What is the name of the British colonial administrator who is credited with starting George Washington's military career?

Q7 George Washington was selected as a delegate to what in 1774?

Q8 The Residence Act, which led to the establishment of Washington D.C., was passed in what year?

Q9 Fort Washington was erected on what island during the American Revolutionary War?

Q10 What conspiracy threatened a military coup against Congress in 1783?

John Adams 1 (easy)

Q1 What was the maiden name of John Adams's wife, Abigail Adams?

    A Johnson
    B Ferguson
    C Smith
    D Washington

Q2 Who served as John Adams's Vice President?

    A Nathanael Greene
    B John Calhoun
    C Aaron Burr
    D Thomas Jefferson

Q3 John Adams served as the first United States ambassador to what two countries?

    A France and Spain
    B France and the United Kingdom
    C United Kingdom and the Netherlands
    D Portugal and Russia

Q4 How many terms did John Adams serve as President?

    A 1
    B 2
    C 3
    D 4

Q5 John Adams was native to what US state?

    A Connecticut
    B Massachusetts
    C Pennsylvania
    D Virginia

Q6 What office did John Adams hold before becoming President?

    A Vice President
    B Senate Majority Leader
    C Speaker of the House of Representatives
    D Governor of Connecticut

Q7 The Treaty of Mortefontaine was signed in 1800 between the USA and what other country?

    A United Kingdom
    B France
    C Spain
    D Russia

Q8 How many children did John Adams have?

    A 0
    B 1
    C 3
    D 6

Q9 How many tie-breaking votes is John Adams believed to have cast?

    A 6
    B 15
    C 29
    D 40

Q10 What warship still in commission today was launched during John Adams's tenure as President?

    A USS *Washington*
    B USS *Monitor*
    C USS *Constitution*
    D USS *Maine*

John Adams 2 (average)

Q1 What political faction did John Adams belong to while he was President?

Q2 Who was John Adams's running mate in the 1796 presidential election?

Q3 John Adams was the first President to reside where?

Q4 What university did John Adams attend?

Q5 What was John Adams's father called?

Q6 John Adams acted as a defence lawyer for British soldiers after what massacre?

Q7 On what frigate did John Adams sail to Europe in 1778?

Q8 What political party did Thomas Jefferson represent in the 1796 presidential election?

Q9 The XYZ Affair triggered what undeclared war?

Q10 The Kentucky and Virginia Resolutions were drafted by what two future presidents?

John Adams 3 (expert)

Q1 John Adams was the primary author of what constitution?

Q2 The controversial Alien and Sedition Acts were passed in what year?

Q3 What textbook was John Adams's early education centred on?

Q4 The Braintree Instructions were written by John Adams in opposition to what?

Q5 Who was on the Committee of Five with John Adams?

Q6 Who swore John Adams into office as President?

Q7 As President, John Adams spent much of his time at what Massachusetts residence?

Q8 What is the name of the Pennsylvania native who organised an armed tax revolt in 1799?

Q9 In what year did John Adams sign the law that established the Library of Congress?

Q10 How old was John Adams when he died?

Thomas Jefferson 1 (easy)

Q1 What territory did the USA purchase off France in 1803?

    A Ohio Territory
    B Indian Territory
    C Oregon Territory
    D Louisiana Territory

Q2 Which US state was Thomas Jefferson a native of?

    A New Hampshire
    B Massachusetts
    C New York
    D Virginia

Q3 How was the First Lady during Thomas Jefferson's tenure as President related to him?

    A Wife
    B Daughter
    C Sister
    D Mother

Q4 Who did Thomas Jefferson's Vice President, Aaron Burr, fatally wound in a duel?

    A George Washington
    B John Adams
    C Alexander Hamilton
    D George III

Q5 As well as being a planter and a politician, what was Thomas Jefferson's main occupation?

    A Lawyer
    B Merchant
    C Military commander
    D Poet

Q6 What post did Thomas Jefferson hold between 1790 and 1793?

    A Vice President
    B Chief Justice of the Supreme Court
    C Governor of South Carolina
    D Secretary of State

Q7 The carving of Thomas Jefferson's face on Mount Rushmore is located in what US state?

    A North Dakota
    B South Dakota
    C Nebraska
    D Washington

Q8 What musical instrument did Thomas Jefferson play from an early age?

    A Trumpet
    B Harp
    C Guitar
    D Violin

Q9 What country supported Thomas Jefferson in his bid to become President in 1796?

    A France
    B Russia
    C United Kingdom
    D Japan

Q10 Thomas Jefferson was a staunch opponent of what United States Secretary of the Treasury?

    A Oliver Wolcott Jr.
    B Alexander Hamilton
    C William Jones
    D Samuel Dexter

Thomas Jefferson 2 (average)

Q1 Thomas Jefferson was a graduate of what college?

Q2 What was the name of Thomas Jefferson's wife?

Q3 What university did Thomas Jefferson found in 1819?

Q4 Thomas Jefferson drafted what 1776 document?

Q5 Maria Cosway – who Thomas Jefferson had a brief romantic relationship with in Paris – was born in what present-day country?

Q6 What newspaper did Thomas Jefferson and James Madison play a key role in founding in 1791?

Q7 Who swore Thomas Jefferson into office as President?

Q8 How many Supreme Court Justices did Thomas Jefferson nominate?

Q9 The Midnight Judges Act concerned what court?

Q10 Which military academy was established in 1802?

Thomas Jefferson 3 (expert)

Q1 Between what years did Thomas Jefferson serve as President?

Q2 What act relating to slaves did Thomas Jefferson sign in 1807?

Q3 What is the name of the only full-length book Thomas Jefferson published during his lifetime?

Q4 What was the name of the slave Thomas Jefferson allegedly had a long-term relationship with?

Q5 How old was Thomas Jefferson when his father, Peter Jefferson, died?

Q6 The Bazeries Cylinder is better known by what name?

Q7 Thomas Jefferson was in Paris when what key event in the French Revolution took place?

Q8 In what year was the first American book on parliamentary procedure, *A Manual of Parliamentary Practice for the Use of the Senate of the United States*, published?

Q9 What war was fought off the coast of Africa between 1801 and 1805?

Q10 What naval engagement took place between the US Navy and the British Royal Navy on 22nd June 1807?

James Madison 1 (easy)

Q1 What position did James Madison hold in Thomas Jefferson's administration?

    A Secretary of State
    B Secretary of War
    C Vice President
    D Secretary of the Treasury

Q2 Who served as Vice President for both Thomas Jefferson and James Madison?

    A Aaron Burr
    B Mike Pence
    C Martin Van Buren
    D George Clinton

Q3 What war did the USA fight against the United Kingdom during James Madison's tenure as President?

    A American Revolutionary War
    B Quasi War
    C War of 1812
    D Seven Years' War

Q4 In what city was the Second Bank of the United States located?

    A New York City
    B Philadelphia
    C Boston
    D Washington D.C.

Q5 James Madison represented what US state in the House of Representatives?

    A New York
    B New Jersey
    C North Carolina
    D Virginia

Q6 What relation was John Payne Todd to James Madison?

A Stepson
B Cousin
C Uncle
D Great grandfather

Q7 The Virginia Statute for Religious Freedom disestablished what church in Virginia?

A Anglican
B Catholic
C Orthodox
D Presbyterian

Q8 James Madison is sometimes hailed as the Father of what?

A America
B Republicanism
C The Constitution
D The Democratic Party

Q9 How many Vice Presidents served under James Madison?

A 0
B 1
C 2
D 3

Q10 Who replaced Robert Smith as Secretary of State in 1811?

A John Quincy Adams
B John Kerry
C James Monroe
D Andrew Jackson

James Madison 2 (average)

Q1 Which two prominent political figures did James Madison co-write *The Federalist Papers* with?

Q2 The Virginia Plan, drafted by James Madison, set the overall agenda for debate at what convention?

Q3 Who did James Madison face in the 1808 presidential election?

Q4 Who was Vice President between 1814 and 1817?

Q5 James Madison is buried in what house's cemetery?

Q6 What was the name of James Madison's wife?

Q7 What university did James Madison study at?

Q8 *Federalist No. 10*, by James Madison, was contained within what collection of essays?

Q9 How many children did James Madison have?

Q10 What political party did James Madison represent as President?

James Madison 3 (expert)

Q1 In what year was the Dallas Tariff passed by Congress?

Q2 What were the names of James Madison's parents?

Q3 The Report of 1800, drafted by James Madison, opposed what acts?

Q4 As the shortest President in the history of the USA, how tall was James Madison?

Q5 What war during James Madison's presidency did some Americans view as being a second war of independence?

Q6 Who did James Madison face in the 1812 presidential election?

Q7 What city was burned by British forces in August 1814?

Q8 The Era of Good Feelings lasted from 1815 until when?

Q9 In what year did James Madison die?

Q10 Which two congressional districts did James Madison represent for Virginia?

James Monroe 1 (easy)

Q1 The Monroe Doctrine was a United States policy opposing European colonisation where?

    A Africa
    B Antarctica
    C The Americas
    D Australia

Q2 James Monroe was the last President of what dynasty?

    A Conservative dynasty
    B Revolutionary dynasty
    C Democratic dynasty
    D Virginia dynasty

Q3 What political party was James Monroe a member of when he served as President?

    A Federalist
    B Know Nothing
    C Democratic-Republican
    D Libertarian

Q4 Who served as James Monroe's Vice President?

    A John C. Calhoun
    B Daniel D. Tompkins
    C Elbridge Gerry
    D Richard M. Johnson

Q5 How was Eliza Monroe Hay related to James Monroe?

    A Daughter
    B Sister
    C Mother
    D Aunt

Q6 What was the Panic of 1819?

    A Period of religious persecution
    B Threat of invasion from Canada
    C Financial crisis
    D Yellow fever outbreak

Q7 The Missouri Compromise was a compromise relating to what issue?

    A Military expenditure
    B Native American territorial claims
    C Religious freedom
    D Slavery

Q8 What African country's capital city is named Monrovia in honour of James Monroe?

    A Nigeria
    B Liberia
    C Ivory Coast
    D Burkina Faso

Q9 James Monroe died in what city?

    A Richmond
    B Philadelphia
    C New York
    D Washington D.C.

Q10 James Monroe died on which American holiday?

    A Thanksgiving
    B Independence Day
    C Presidents' Day
    D Labor Day

James Monroe 2 (average)

Q1 James Monroe was wounded during what battle in 1776?

Q2 How many times did James Monroe serve as Governor of Virginia?

Q3 Who did James Monroe face in the 1816 presidential election?

Q4 What was the name of James Monroe's wife?

Q5 James Monroe was the last President to serve during what party system?

Q6 What did the USA acquire in the Adams–Onís Treaty of 1819?

Q7 What college did James Monroe attend?

Q8 Ash Lawn–Highland – an estate owned by James Monroe – was located near what city?

Q9 How many terms did James Monroe serve as President?

Q10 The Rush–Bagot Treaty was a treaty between the USA and what other country?

James Monroe 3 (expert)

Q1 In what year was the Monroe Doctrine issued?

Q2 What was the name of James Monroe's uncle, who acted as a surrogate father following the death of his biological father?

Q3 What was the maiden name of James Monroe's wife?

Q4 James Monroe served as an ambassador to what two countries?

Q5 James Monroe recognised the independence of which 5 countries in 1822?

Q6 What political party failed to put forward a presidential candidate for the first time in the 1820 presidential election?

Q7 How many states were admitted to the Union during James Monroe's presidency?

Q8 What state did Maine secede from in 1820?

Q9 James Monroe was elected as a delegate to what convention, held between 1829 and 1830?

Q10 In what year was the General Survey Act passed?

John Quincy Adams 1 (easy)

Q1 What relation was John Adams to John Quincy Adams?

    A Uncle
    B Father
    C Grandfather
    D Brother

Q2 John Quincy Adams was a native of what US state?

    A Virginia
    B Pennsylvania
    C Massachusetts
    D New Jersey

Q3 John C. Calhoun served as Vice President under how many Presidents?

    A 0
    B 1
    C 2
    D 3

Q4 How many members of the Democratic-Republican Party competed for the presidency in the 1824 presidential election?

    A 1
    B 2
    C 4
    D 7

Q5 Who won the 1828 presidential election?

    A John C. Calhoun
    B Martin Van Buren
    C John Quincy Adams
    D Andrew Jackson

Q6 How many countries did John Quincy Adams serve as an ambassador to?

A 1
B 2
C 3
D 4

Q7 What was the name of John Quincy Adams's wife?

A Helen Adams
B Amy Adams
C Martha Adams
D Louisa Adams

Q8 How many children did John Quincy Adams have?

A 0
B 2
C 4
D 9

Q9 In what major city was John Quincy Adams's wife born?

A London
B Paris
C New York
D Philadelphia

Q10 What type of book did John Quincy Adams take the oath of office on?

A Bible
B Law book
C Blank book
D Biography of John Adams

John Quincy Adams 2 (average)

Q1 How many terms did John Quincy Adams serve as President?

Q2 What did John Quincy Adams serve as between 1831 and 1848?

Q3 Who was John Quincy Adams named after?

Q4 What university did John Quincy Adams attend?

Q5 John Quincy Adams declined an offer to become what in 1811?

Q6 What position did John Quincy Adams hold in James Monroe's administration?

Q7 As well as John Quincy Adams, which Kentucky congressman was a supporter of the American System?

Q8 John Quincy Adams and which other President is buried at United First Parish Church?

Q9 John Quincy Adams was nicknamed Old Man what?

Q10 John Quincy Adams was the first President who wasn't a Founding what?

John Quincy Adams 3 (expert)

Q1 In 1824 John Quincy Adams became the first person to win a presidential election despite losing what?

Q2 In what church did John Quincy Adams get married?

Q3 John Quincy Adams opposed the impeachment of which Supreme Court Justice in 1803?

Q4 What position did Samuel L. Southard hold in John Quincy Adams's administration?

Q5 In what year was the Congress of Panama held?

Q6 As Secretary of State, what doctrine did John Quincey Adams famously compose?

Q7 What position did John Adams appoint John Quincy Adams to?

Q8 In 1814, John Quincy Adams was part of the delegation which negotiated the treaty ending the War of 1812. Which treaty was this?

Q9 What 1841 Supreme Court case was John Quincy Adams involved in?

Q10 John Quincy Adams was a key driving force behind the establishment of what institution in 1846?

Andrew Jackson 1 (easy)

Q1 Andrew Jackson served as a senator for what US state?

    A Virginia
    B South Carolina
    C Georgia
    D Tennessee

Q2 How many people served as First Lady during Andrew Jackson's presidency?

    A 0
    B 1
    C 2
    D 3

Q3 In what year did Andrew Jackson first run for President?

    A 1816
    B 1824
    C 1828
    D 1836

Q4 Andrew Jackson was the first President from what political party?

    A Democratic
    B Republican
    C Whig
    D Libertarian

Q5 The Nullification Crisis involved a confrontation between the Jackson administration and what US state?

    A Alabama
    B Mississippi
    C North Carolina
    D South Carolina

Q6 The forced relocation of Native peoples from their homelands in the south-eastern United States was known as the Trail of what?

A Arrows
B Tyranny
C Tears
D Destiny

Q7 What present-day country were Andrew Jackson's parents from?

A Belgium
B Wales
C Northern Ireland
D Canada

Q8 Andrew Jackson was trained as a what?

A Architect
B Sailor
C Lawyer
D Blacksmith

Q9 Andrew Jackson was nicknamed Old what?

A President
B Warhorse
C Hickory
D Frontier-man

Q10 The French pirate Jean Lafitte helped Andrew Jackson defend what city?

A St Augustine
B New Orleans
C New York
D Memphis

Andrew Jackson 2 (average)

Q1 What was the name of Andrew Jackson's wife?

Q2 Which two politicians served as Vice President during Andrew Jackson's presidency?

Q3 How many terms did Andrew Jackson serve as President?

Q4 The Hermitage – a plantation owned by Andrew Jackson – is located near what city?

Q5 Andrew Jackson's victory at what battle during the War of 1812 made him a national hero?

Q6 The Bank War refers to a political struggle concerning the re-chartering of which bank?

Q7 The Indian Removal Act called for Native American tribes living in the south-eastern United States to be removed west of what river?

Q8 What newly-formed republic did the USA recognise in 1837?

Q9 Andrew Jackson fought against what two countries at the Battle of Pensacola?

Q10 What type of crisis hit the USA in 1837?

Andrew Jackson 3 (expert)

Q1 In what war was the Battle of Horseshoe Bend fought?

Q2 The Tariff of 1828 was given what other name by its critics?

Q3 In what year was the Indian Removal Act signed?

Q4 Prior to marrying Andrew Jackson, who was his wife married to?

Q5 The Jackson Purchase is a region covering parts of what two US states?

Q6 Andrew Jackson won the popular vote in how many presidential elections?

Q7 Andrew Jackson's family were members of what religious denomination?

Q8 What was the name of the series of pamphlets that attacked Andrew Jackson during the 1828 presidential election?

Q9 Who attempted to assassinate Andrew Jackson in 1835?

Q10 Who swore Andrew Jackson into office as President?

Martin Van Buren 1 (easy)

Q1 How many terms did Martin Van Buren serve as President?

    A 1
    B 2
    C 3
    D 4

Q2 Martin Van Buren was a member of what political party during his tenure as President?

    A Democratic-Republican
    B Democratic
    C Whig
    D Republican

Q3 Martin Van Buren served as Governor of what US state?

    A Virginia
    B New York
    C Pennsylvania
    D Tennessee

Q4 What was the name of Martin Van Buren's wife?

    A Dana Van Buren
    B Hannah Van Buren
    C Ethel Van Buren
    D Georgina Van Buren

Q5 What position did Martin Van Buren hold prior to becoming President?

    A Vice President
    B Senate Minority Leader
    C Speaker of the House of Representatives
    D Secretary of War

Q6 Martin Van Buren's family originated from what country?

A Germany
B France
C United Kingdom
D The Netherlands

Q7 Martin Van Buren was nicknamed Little what?

A Magician
B Dutchman
C Foot
D Mercy

Q8 Martin Van Buren opposed the annexation of what future US state?

A Hawaii
B Alaska
C Oregon
D Texas

Q9 How many children did Martin Van Buren have?

A 0
B 2
C 5
D 17

Q10 How many Supreme Court Justices did Martin Van Buren nominate?

A 0
B 1
C 2
D 5

Martin Van Buren 2 (average)

Q1 What relation was Sarah Angelica Van Buren to Martin Van Buren?

Q2 Martin Van Buren represented what party in the 1848 presidential election?

Q3 Who served as Vice President during Martin Van Buren's presidency?

Q4 Martin Van Buren was the first President not to have been born a subject of...

Q5 Which side did Martin Van Buren support in the American Civil War?

Q6 Who served as Secretary of State during Martin Van Buren's presidency?

Q7 William Henry Harrison, who defeated Martin Van Buren in the 1840 presidential election, represented what political party?

Q8 What war was fought in Florida between 1835 and 1842?

Q9 *United States v. The Amistad* was a Supreme Court case concerning a slave rebellion on board a schooner owned by what country?

Q10 What was Martin Van Buren's second language?

Martin Van Buren 3 (expert)

Q1 What was the name of Martin Van Buren's eldest son?

Q2 What group of politicians was Martin Van Buren involved with between 1822 and 1838?

Q3 Martin Van Buren is buried in the graveyard of what church?

Q4 How many Whig Party candidates were there in the 1836 presidential election?

Q5 The Gold Spoon Oration was a political speech given by who?

Q6 Which Missouri Governor issued an 'Extermination Order' against the Mormons during Martin Van Buren's presidency?

Q7 Which room in the White House has traditionally retained the same colour decor that was chosen for it by Martin Van Buren in 1837?

Q8 Who was Martin Van Buren's running mate in the 1840 presidential election?

Q9 Martin Van Buren served as Secretary of State for what President?

Q10 Martin Van Buren held his first position in the federal government during what era?

William Henry Harrison 1 (easy)

Q1 How long did William Henry Harrison serve as President?

    A 1 week
    B 1 month
    C 1 year
    D 4 years

Q2 What political party was William Henry Harrison a member of during his tenure as President?

    A Whig
    B Democrat
    C Know Nothing
    D Republican

Q3 William Henry Harrison served as Governor of what territory?

    A Ohio Territory
    B Oregon Territory
    C Indiana Territory
    D Indian Territory

Q4 Who served as First Lady during William Henry Harrison's presidency?

    A Brenda Harrison
    B Anna Harrison
    C Mildred Harrison
    D Jane Harrison

Q5 What did William Henry Harrison die from?

    A Heart attack
    B Pneumonia
    C Asthma attack
    D Gunshot wound

Q6 What university did William Henry Harrison attend?

    A Harvard University
    B Notre Dame University
    C University of Pennsylvania
    D Yale University

Q7 William Henry Harrison was a native of what US state?

    A New Hampshire
    B Rhode Island
    C Connecticut
    D Virginia

Q8 William Henry Harrison was nicknamed Old what?

    A Tippecanoe
    B School
    C Glory
    D Rider

Q9 Which Congress sat during William Henry Harrison's presidency?

    A 12th
    B 27th
    C 39th
    D 42nd

Q10 William Henry Harrison served as ambassador to what country between 1828 and 1829?

    A Gran Colombia
    B Mexico
    C Haiti
    D United Kingdom

William Henry Harrison 2 (average)

Q1 William Henry Harrison was born on what plantation?

Q2 Which President was the grandson of William Henry Harrison?

Q3 Who served as William Henry Harrison's Vice President?

Q4 What event is believed to have caused William Henry Harrison's death?

Q5 Who swore William Henry Harrison into office?

Q6 What did William Henry Harrison abandon in favour of pursuing a military career?

Q7 During what war did William Henry Harrison lead his troops to victory at the Battle of the Thames?

Q8 William Henry Harrison was the last President to have been born before what conflict?

Q9 William Henry Harrison's mansion Grouseland is situated in which US state?

Q10 Who served as Secretary of State during William Henry Harrison's presidency?

William Henry Harrison 3 (expert)

Q1 What was *Tippecanoe and Tyler Too*?

Q2 William Henry Harrison was the son of which Founding Father?

Q3 In what chapel did William Henry Harrison's funeral take place?

Q4 How many people served as President in 1841?

Q5 What memorial was erected in North Bend, Ohio in William Henry Harrison's honour?

Q6 What was William Henry Harrison's wife's maiden name?

Q7 William Henry Harrison was aide-de-camp of what army officer?

Q8 William Henry Harrison founded what university?

Q9 In what year was the Treaty of Fort Wayne signed?

Q10 William Henry Harrison commanded what army during the War of 1812?

John Tyler 1 (easy)

Q1 How many terms did John Tyler serve as President?

    A 1
    B 2
    C 3
    D 4

Q2 What position did John Tyler hold prior to becoming President?

    A Speaker of the House of Representatives
    B Governor of New Hampshire
    C Vice President
    D Attorney General

Q3 John Tyler was a native of what US state?

    A North Carolina
    B South Carolina
    C Georgia
    D Virginia

Q4 How many people served as First Lady during John Tyler's presidency?

    A 0
    B 1
    C 2
    D 3

Q5 What relation was Priscilla Cooper Tyler to John Tyler?

    A Wife
    B Mother
    C Daughter-in-law
    D Step sister

Q6 What was John Tyler's nickname?

    A Father of Virginia
    B His Accidency
    C The Texan
    D Mr Miracle

Q7 What political party did John Tyler belong to when he became President?

    A Free Soil
    B Know Nothing
    C Democratic
    D Whig

Q8 What profession was John Tyler trained in?

    A Engineering
    B Law
    C Sailing
    D Mining

Q9 What was John Tyler's military rank during the War of 1812?

    A Major General
    B Brigadier
    C Captain
    D Colonel

Q10 Who did not resign from John Tyler's Cabinet when he vetoed legislation for a national banking act?

    A Daniel Webster
    B Thomas Ewing
    C John Bell
    D George E. Badger

John Tyler 2 (average)

Q1 Which side did John Tyler support in the American Civil War?

Q2 Letitia Christian Tyler was the first First Lady to die where?

Q3 John Tyler was reared on what plantation?

Q4 What college did John Tyler attend?

Q5 A number of high-ranking federal government officials were killed by an explosion on board what ship in 1844?

Q6 What did John Tyler rename his plantation in Charles City County, Virginia?

Q7 Who served as Vice President during John Tyler's presidency?

Q8 John Tyler was expelled from what political party?

Q9 The Webster–Ashburton Treaty settled border disputes between the USA and…

Q10 John Tyler pursued the annexation of what republic?

John Tyler 3 (expert)

Q1 John Tyler is buried in what Richmond cemetery?

Q2 What were the names of John Tyler's two wives?

Q3 John Tyler died during what war?

Q4 How old was John Tyler when his mother died?

Q5 For his military service in the War of 1812, John Tyler was granted land near what city?

Q6 What was the name of the only person John Tyler successfully nominated to be a Supreme Court Justice?

Q7 What were John Tyler's last words?

Q8 John Tyler is buried near which other President?

Q9 Who was the Whig candidate in the 1844 presidential election?

Q10 What two meetings of Congress took place during John Tyler's presidency?

James Polk 1 (easy)

Q1 James Polk was a member of what political party during his presidency?

    A Republican
    B Democratic
    C Whig
    D Libertarian

Q2 What was the name of James Polk's father?

    A Samuel Polk
    B Andrew Polk
    C Marcus Polk
    D William Polk

Q3 James Polk served as Governor of what US state?

    A Rhode Island
    B Massachusetts
    C Virginia
    D Tennessee

Q4 How many times did James Polk marry?

    A 0
    B 1
    C 2
    D 3

Q5 James Polk was sometimes referred to as Young what?

    A Soldier
    B Patriot
    C Hickory
    D Stallion

Q6 How long after leaving office did James Polk die?

    A Less than a year
    B 2 years
    C 10 years
    D 40 years

Q7 Who served as James Polk's Vice President?

    A Millard Fillmore
    B John C. Calhoun
    C James Buchanan
    D George M. Dallas

Q8 What war took place during James Polk's presidency?

    A Spanish-American War
    B Mexican-American War
    C War of 1812
    D American Civil War

Q9 Which of these states was not admitted to the union during James Polk's presidency?

    A Texas
    B Wisconsin
    C Oregon
    D Iowa

Q10 In what year did James W. Marshall discover gold in California?

    A 1830
    B 1844
    C 1848
    D 1850

James Polk 2 (average)

Q1 How many terms did James Polk serve as President?

Q2 Who served as First Lady during James Polk's presidency?

Q3 James Polk was born in what US state?

Q4 What was James Polk's middle name?

Q5 James Polk was a protégé of which President?

Q6 Who did James Polk defeat in the 1844 presidential election?

Q7 'Fifty-four forty or fight!' was a campaign pledge by James Polk to take complete control of what territory?

Q8 James Polk attended what university?

Q9 How many children did James Polk have?

Q10 Who served as Secretary of State during James Polk's presidency?

James Polk 3 (expert)

Q1 The Oregon Treaty was signed in what year?

Q2 Where was James Polk's body moved to in 1893?

Q3 How many siblings did James Polk have?

Q4 What is James Polk believed to have died from?

Q5 The Walker Tariff made substantial cuts to what 1842 tariff?

Q6 The Independent Treasury was created by which Congress?

Q7 In what year did James Polk become Speaker of the House of Representatives?

Q8 Why didn't James Polk stand for re-election in the 1848 presidential election?

Q9 How many people did James Polk successfully appoint as Supreme Court Justices?

Q10 The home of James Polk, Polk Place, was located in what city?

Zachary Taylor 1 (easy)

Q1 How long did Zachary Taylor serve as President?

    A 2 months
    B 16 months
    C 3 years
    D 5 years

Q2 What was Zachary Taylor's wife called?

    A Margaret Taylor
    B Debbie Taylor
    C Margaret Taylor
    D Elizabeth Taylor

Q3 What US state was Zachary Taylor born in?

    A Mississippi
    B Pennsylvania
    C Virginia
    D New Jersey

Q4 What political party was Zachary Taylor a member of during his presidency?

    A Whig
    B Democratic
    C Know Nothing
    D Libertarian

Q5 What did Zachary Taylor name one of his horses?

    A Noble Steed
    B Buckaroo
    C Old Whitey
    D Brown

Q6 The Compromise of 1850 was centred on what issue?

A Voting rights
B Military expenditure
C Tax
D Slavery

Q7 What was Zachary Taylor's occupation?

A Soldier
B Lawyer
C Engineer
D Journalist

Q8 The Clayton–Bulwer Treaty was a treaty between the USA and what other country?

A France
B United Kingdom
C Mexico
D The Netherlands

Q9 Zachary Taylor commanded the Army of Occupation during what war?

A Mexican-American War
B War of 1812
C Second Seminole War
D American Civil War

Q10 How many Supreme Court Justices did Zachary Taylor appoint?

A 0
B 1
C 2
D 3

Zachary Taylor 2 (average)

Q1 What was Zachary Taylor's nickname?

Q2 Who served as Vice President during Zachary Taylor's presidency?

Q3 What elected political office did Zachary Taylor hold before becoming president?

Q4 Who was Zachary Taylor's main opponent in the 1848 presidential election?

Q5 Who was Zachary Taylor's father?

Q6 Zachary Taylor is buried at a cemetery in what city?

Q7 Which former President ran unsuccessfully in the 1848 presidential election?

Q8 John Middleton Clayton held what position in Zachary Taylor's administration?

Q9 The State of Deseret was located in what present-day US state?

Q10 The Treaty of Guadalupe Hidalgo was agreed between the USA and what other country?

Zachary Taylor 3 (expert)

Q1 Zachary Taylor was a descendant of what passenger on the *Mayflower*?

Q2 What rank did Zachary Taylor hold in the army when he became President?

Q3 In what year was the Clayton–Bulwer Treaty ratified?

Q4 How many children did Zachary Taylor have?

Q5 The Galphin Affair involved what member of Zachary Taylor's cabinet?

Q6 In what year did the US Post Office release the first Zachary Taylor stamp?

Q7 John J. Crittenden declined Zachary Taylor's offer to serve as Secretary of State in order to finish his term as what?

Q8 Zachary Taylor was picked up by the steamer *Saladin* after being elected President. But which steamer was he supposed to be picked up by?

Q9 Zachary Taylor was President during what party system?

Q10 The Wilmot Proviso was an unsuccessful proposal to ban what from territory acquired from Mexico?

Millard Fillmore 1 (easy)

Q1 Millard Fillmore was the last President to represent what political party?

    A Democratic-Republican
    B Whig
    C Libertarian
    D Federalist

Q2 What position did Millard Fillmore hold before becoming President?

    A Speaker of the House of Representatives
    B Senate Majority Leader
    C Secretary of State
    D Vice President

Q3 Millard Fillmore was born in what US state?

    A New York
    B New Jersey
    C Pennsylvania
    D Vermont

Q4 How many times did Millard Fillmore marry?

    A 0
    B 1
    C 2
    D 3

Q5 Who served as First Lady during Millard Fillmore's tenure as President?

    A Jane Fillmore
    B Mary Fillmore
    C Abigail Fillmore
    D Clara Fillmore

Q6 What was Millard Fillmore's profession?

    A Actor
    B Teacher
    C Lawyer
    D Merchant

Q7 What state was admitted to the Union during Millard Fillmore's presidency?

    A California
    B Minnesota
    C Illinois
    D Michigan

Q8 How many children did Millard Fillmore have?

    A 0
    B 2
    C 5
    D 14

Q9 Who won the 1856 presidential election?

    A James Buchanan
    B Millard Fillmore
    C Abraham Lincoln
    D John C Fremont

Q10 Millard Fillmore declined an honorary degree from what university?

    A Yale University
    B Oxford University
    C Princeton University
    D Harvard University

Millard Fillmore 2 (average)

Q1 Who served as Vice President during Millard Fillmore's presidency?

Q2 Millard Fillmore was elected President in how many presidential elections?

Q3 What judge did Millard Fillmore successfully appoint to the Supreme Court?

Q4 Millard Fillmore was elected to what position in 1847?

Q5 Who did Millard Fillmore send to Japan with the intention of opening up trade?

Q6 Millard Fillmore had an audience with which Pope?

Q7 What position did Daniel Webster hold when he died in office?

Q8 Who swore Millard Fillmore in as President?

Q9 Who was the Whig Party candidate in the 1852 presidential election?

Q10 In what year was the Fugitive Slave Act passed?

Millard Fillmore 3 (expert)

Q1 In what cemetery is Millard Fillmore buried?

Q2 What political party did Millard Fillmore represent in the 1856 presidential election?

Q3 In what year was Millard Fillmore born?

Q4 In what years did Millard Fillmore serve as President?

Q5 How many individuals served as Secretary of State during Millard Fillmore's presidency?

Q6 Narciso López was executed on what island?

Q7 Millard Fillmore served as the first chancellor of what university?

Q8 Fillmore House is located in what village?

Q9 Who did Millard Fillmore appoint as the first Governor of Utah Territory?

Q10 Who did Millard Fillmore support in the 1864 presidential election?

Franklin Pierce 1 (easy)

Q1 Franklin Pierce was a member of what political party during his presidency?

    A Democratic
    B Republican
    C Know Nothing
    D Whigs

Q2 How many children did Franklin Pierce have?

    A 0
    B 3
    C 7
    D 10

Q3 What was Franklin Pierce's wife called?

    A Mandy Pierce
    B Jennie Pierce
    C Robyn Pierce
    D Jane Pierce

Q4 In what year was the Kansas–Nebraska Act passed?

    A 1849
    B 1854
    C 1856
    D 1860

Q5 Franklin Pierce was born in what US state?

    A New Hampshire
    B New York
    C New Jersey
    D Rhode Island

Q6 William Rufus DeVane King held what position in Franklin Pierce's administration?

    A Vice President
    B Secretary of State
    C Secretary of War
    D Attorney General

Q7 How was Benjamin Kendrick Pierce related to Franklin Pierce?

    A Father
    B Son
    C Brother
    D Great grandfather

Q8 Who did Franklin Pierce face in the 1852 presidential election?

    A Stephen Douglas
    B Ulysses Grant
    C James Buchanan
    D Winfield Scott

Q9 Franklin Pierce was a close friend of which novelist?

    A Mark Twain
    B Nathaniel Hawthorne
    C Washington Irving
    D Harriet Beecher Stowe

Q10 Who served as Secretary of War during Franklin Pierce's presidency?

    A Stephen Douglas
    B John C Fremont
    C Jefferson Davis
    D Winfield Scott

Franklin Pierce 2 (average)

Q1 How many terms did Franklin Pierce serve as President?

Q2 Who served as Vice President between April 1853 and March 1857?

Q3 What was Franklin Pierce's occupation before he became President?

Q4 Franklin Pierce's father served as Governor of what US state?

Q5 What position did William Marcy hold in Franklin Pierce's administration?

Q6 The Gadsden Purchase led to the USA acquiring land in what two present-day US states?

Q7 Which Senator drafted the Kansas–Nebraska Act with Franklin Pierce?

Q8 Franklin Pierce recognised William Walker as President of what country?

Q9 Who defeated Franklin Pierce at the 1856 Democratic National Convention?

Q10 What name was given to the series of violent civil confrontations that occurred in Kansas and Missouri between 1854 and 1861?

Franklin Pierce 3 (expert)

Q1 In what battle was Franklin Pierce injured while riding his horse?

Q2 What college did Franklin Pierce attend?

Q3 On what number ballot did Franklin Pierce win the 1852 Democratic nomination for president?

Q4 Where did Franklin Pierce's Vice President take the oath of office?

Q5 Franklin Pierce is buried in what cemetery?

Q6 What condition did Franklin Pierce die from?

Q7 What accident caused the death of 11-year-old Benjamin Pierce shortly after Franklin Pierce became President?

Q8 The Koszta Affair was a diplomatic episode between the USA and which empire?

Q9 During the American Civil War the *Detroit Tribune* accused Franklin Pierce of being a member of what secret society?

Q10 The Ostend Manifesto discussed the possibility of annexing what island?

James Buchanan 1 (easy)

Q1 James Buchanan was nicknamed Old what?

    A Big Nose
    B Patriot
    C Southerner
    D Buck

Q2 What political party was James Buchanan a member of during his presidency?

    A Democratic
    B Republican
    C Know Nothing
    D Libertarian

Q3 What relation was Harriet Lane to James Buchanan?

    A Sister
    B Cousin
    C Niece
    D Step daughter

Q4 James Buchanan served as President immediately prior to what war?

    A Spanish-American War
    B American Civil War
    C Mexican-American War
    D Second Seminole War

Q5 James Buchanan was born in what US state?

    A New York
    B Ohio
    C Indiana
    D Pennsylvania

Q6 What position did James Buchanan hold during Franklin Pierce's presidency?

A Ambassador to the United Kingdom
B Associate Justice of the Supreme Court
C Secretary of State
D Attorney General

Q7 How many proposed constitutions were there for Kansas?

A 1
B 4
C 5
D 9

Q8 What was the Panic of 1857?

A Slave uprising
B Financial crisis
C Smallpox epidemic
D Arms race

Q9 What city did James Buchanan help defend during the War of 1812?

A Washington D.C.
B Baltimore
C Philadelphia
D Des Moines

Q10 Which member of James Buchanan's cabinet also served in Abraham Lincoln's cabinet?

A Aaron Brown
B Edwin Stanton
C Howell Cobb
D Horatio King

James Buchanan 2 (average)

Q1 How many terms did James Buchanan serve as President?

Q2 Who served as James Buchanan's Vice President?

Q3 How many times did James Buchanan marry?

Q4 James Buchanan attended what college?

Q5 James Buchanan began his political career as a member of what party?

Q6 Which President appointed James Buchanan Secretary of State?

Q7 Which judge did James Buchanan successfully appoint as a Supreme Court Justice?

Q8 The Mountain Meadows Massacre occurred in what US territory?

Q9 How many states were admitted to the Union during James Buchanan's presidency?

Q10 Who swore James Buchanan into office as President?

James Buchanan 3 (expert)

Q1 In what year was the Dred Scott decision made by the Supreme Court?

Q2 Which two candidates did James Buchanan defeat in the 1856 presidential election?

Q3 Which four political parties competed for office in the 1860 presidential election?

Q4 James Buchanan is buried in which cemetery?

Q5 Who was James Buchanan engaged to in 1819?

Q6 James Buchanan's house 'Wheatland' was located near which city?

Q7 In which city was the 1856 Democratic National Convention held?

Q8 James Buchanan served as Ambassador to Russia during which President's administration?

Q9 What rank did James Buchanan hold in the army?

Q10 In which city was the 1860 Democratic National Convention initially held?

Abraham Lincoln 1 (easy)

Q1 Who assassinated Abraham Lincoln?

    A Leon Czolgosz
    B Charles Wilkes Booth
    C Richard Lawrence
    D Lee Harvey Oswald

Q2 Abraham Lincoln was the first President from what political party?

    A Democratic
    B Republican
    C Libertarian
    D Know Nothing

Q3 Abraham Lincoln was born in what US state?

    A Illinois
    B New York
    C Kentucky
    D Indiana

Q4 How many Vice Presidents served during Abraham Lincoln's presidency?

    A 0
    B 1
    C 2
    D 4

Q5 After what battle was the Emancipation Proclamation issued?

    A Gettysburg
    B Antietam
    C Shiloh
    D Fredericksburg

Q6 The Lincoln–Douglas debates took place in what year?

A 1840
B 1850
C 1858
D 1864

Q7 Who served as President of the Confederate States of America?

A Judah Benjamin
B Jefferson Davis
C Alexander Stephens
D Robert E Lee

Q8 At its height, how many states were there in the Confederate States of America?

A 3
B 7
C 11
D 15

Q9 What state split into two states in the American Civil War?

A Maine
B Virginia
C Kentucky
D Tennessee

Q10 What was Abraham Lincoln's occupation?

A Lawyer
B Author
C Merchant
D Lumberjack

Abraham Lincoln 2 (average)

Q1 Abraham Lincoln served as a Congressman representing what US state?

Q2 Abraham Lincoln was assassinated at what theatre?

Q3 What was the name of Abraham Lincoln's wife?

Q4 Who was Abraham Lincoln's running mate in the 1860 presidential election?

Q5 How many times was Abraham Lincoln elected President?

Q6 Who did Abraham Lincoln successfully appoint as Chief Justice of the United States?

Q7 What position did William Seward hold during Abraham Lincoln's presidency?

Q8 Abraham Lincoln served as a captain in what war?

Q9 The Baltimore Plot of 1861 was an alleged plot to do what?

Q10 Who proposed the Anaconda Plan?

Abraham Lincoln 3 (expert)

Q1 Which of Abraham Lincoln's children died during the American Civil War?

Q2 Abraham Lincoln is buried in what cemetery?

Q3 What diplomatic incident in 1861 threatened was between the USA and the United Kingdom?

Q4 Who was allegedly Abraham Lincoln's first love?

Q5 In what year did Abraham Lincoln deliver the Gettysburg Address?

Q6 Who served as Speaker of the House of Representatives between 1861 and 1863?

Q7 What era of American history began during Abraham Lincoln's presidency?

Q8 In what year was the first of the Homestead Acts passed?

Q9 The Pacific Railroad Acts promoted the construction of what?

Q10 Abraham Lincoln gave the Cooper Union speech in what city?

Andrew Johnson 1 (easy)

Q1 What name did the Republican Party temporarily adopt during the 1864 presidential election?

    A American Party
    B Unionist Party
    C National Union Party
    D Counterrevolutionary Party

Q2 On how many occasions was Andrew Johnson elected President?

    A 0
    B 1
    C 2
    D 3

Q3 Andrew Johnson served as the Governor of what US state?

    A Tennessee
    B North Carolina
    C Florida
    D New Jersey

Q4 What city was Andrew Johnson born in?

    A Raleigh
    B Memphis
    C Newark
    D Detroit

Q5 How long did Andrew Johnson serve as Abraham Lincoln's Vice President?

    A 1 day
    B Under 2 months
    C 18 months
    D 4 years

Q6 In what year was Andrew Johnson impeached?

A 1865
B 1868
C 1870
D 1872

Q7 What was Andrew Johnson's profession?

A Tailor
B Lawyer
C Architect
D Farmer

Q8 What amendment to the United States Constitution was adopted in 1868?

A 13th
B 14th
C 15th
D 16th

Q9 The Tenure of Office Act (1867) sought to limit whose power?

A President
B Supreme Court
C Congress
D States

Q10 Andrew Johnson's father died as a result of what?

A Cholera
B Wounds sustained in the War of 1812
C Saving two men from drowning
D Suicide

Andrew Johnson 2 (average)

Q1 What was the name of Andrew Johnson's wife?

Q2 What political party was Andrew Johnson a member of?

Q3 Who did Andrew Johnson attempt to replace Edwin Stanton with as Secretary of War?

Q4 Who presided over the Senate trial of Andrew Johnson during his impeachment proceedings?

Q5 Who did Andrew Johnson replace as Abraham Lincoln's Vice President?

Q6 Whose job was it to assassinate Andrew Johnson on the night Abraham Lincoln was killed?

Q7 What political office did Andrew Johnson hold after leaving the presidency?

Q8 What did Andrew Johnson die from?

Q9 What territory did Andrew Johnson veto being granted statehood in 1865?

Q10 Andrew Johnson served as President during what era in American history?

Andrew Johnson 3 (expert)

Q1 In what years were the Black Codes passed?

Q2 How many members of the House of Representatives voted in favour of impeaching Andrew Johnson?

Q3 Which Kansas Senator voted against convicting Andrew Johnson of 'high crimes and misdemeanours'?

Q4 On what date did Andrew Johnson's inauguration as President take place?

Q5 As well as Abraham Lincoln and Andrew Johnson, which other government official did conspirators attempt to assassinate at the end of the American Civil War?

Q6 Andrew Johnson is buried in a cemetery in what town?

Q7 How many children did Andrew Johnson have?

Q8 What university was Andrew Johnson a graduate of?

Q9 What faction of the Democratic Party was Andrew Johnson associated with during the American Civil War?

Q10 What was Andrew Johnson's military rank during the American Civil War?

Ulysses Grant 1 (easy)

Q1 What Christian name was given to Ulysses Grant when he was born?

    A Geoffrey
    B Hiram
    C Bryan
    D Daniel

Q2 Ulysses Grant was born in what US state?

    A Mississippi
    B Ohio
    C Pennsylvania
    D Maine

Q3 What was the name of Ulysses Grant's wife?

    A Dana Grant
    B Emily Grant
    C Mary-Jayne Grant
    D Julia Grant

Q4 What was the first national park in the USA?

    A Acadia
    B Grand Canyon
    C Yosemite
    D Yellowstone

Q5 What amendment to the United States Constitution was passed during Ulysses Grant's presidency?

    A 13th
    B 14th
    C 15th
    D 16th

Q6 What did Ulysses Grant do after his presidency ended?

A Embark on a world tour
B Unsuccessfully run to become a Senator
C Return to military service
D Become a university professor

Q7 In what city did Ulysses Grant get married?

A Denver, Colorado
B St Louis, Missouri
C Columbus, Ohio
D Minneapolis, Minnesota

Q8 In what year did Ulysses Grant become Commanding General of the United States Army?

A 1858
B 1861
C 1864
D 1867

Q9 Who did Ulysses Grant face in the 1868 presidential election?

A George Brinton McClellan
B Andrew Johnson
C Horatio Seymour
D Horace Greeley

Q10 Who served as Secretary of State for the majority of Ulysses Grant's presidency?

A Mike Pompeo
B Hamilton Fish
C William Maxwell Evarts
D William Seward

Ulysses Grant 2 (average)

Q1 How many terms did Ulysses Grant serve as President?

Q2 What military academy did Ulysses Grant attend?

Q3 What political party was Ulysses Grant a member of during his presidency?

Q4 Where did Robert E Lee surrender to Ulysses Grant?

Q5 In what year did the Battle of Fort Donelson take place?

Q6 Ulysses Grant's first Secretary of State served just 11 days before he resigned to become the USA's ambassador to France. Who was he?

Q7 The father of which President served as Secretary of War and Attorney General during Ulysses Grant's presidency?

Q8 The Crédit Mobilier scandal involved what railroad?

Q9 A fire devastated what city in 1871?

Q10 What was the only state to be admitted to the Union during Ulysses Grant's presidency?

Ulysses Grant 3 (expert)

Q1 What two individuals served as Vice President during Ulysses Grant's tenure as President?

Q2 In what year was the USA's first national park created?

Q3 Ulysses Grant's ancestors Matthew and Priscilla Grant arrived in the Americas on board what ship?

Q4 Horace Greeley – Ulysses Grant's main opponent in the 1872 presidential election – represented what political party?

Q5 Which three states were excluded from the 1868 presidential election?

Q6 How many judges did Ulysses Grant successfully appoint to the Supreme Court?

Q7 What business partner left Ulysses Grant almost penniless in 1884?

Q8 Who was the sponsor of Ulysses Grant's memoirs?

Q9 In what year was the United States Department of Justice formed?

Q10 The United States demanded damages from which country in the *Alabama* Claims?

Rutherford Hayes 1 (easy)

Q1 What was Rutherford Hayes's middle name?

    A Pritchard
    B Birchard
    C Drew
    D Samuel

Q2 What was the name of Rutherford Hayes's wife?

    A Lucy
    B Sarah
    C Danielle
    D Sandra

Q3 What US state was Rutherford Hayes born in?

    A Missouri
    B Illinois
    C Massachusetts
    D Ohio

Q4 Who did Rutherford Hayes defeat in the 1876 presidential election?

    A Ulysses Grant
    B Robert E Lee
    C Samuel Tilden
    D Grover Cleveland

Q5 Rutherford Hayes was seriously wounded in what battle?

    A Battle of South Mountain
    B Battle of Fredericksburg
    C Battle of Pea Ridge
    D Second Battle of Bull Run

Q6 In the Compromise of 1877, Rutherford Hayes was awarded the White House on the understanding that he would do what?

    A Keep Washington D.C. as the USA's capital city
    B Pull remaining federal troops out of the South
    C Have his opponent as Vice President
    D Protect states' rights

Q7 Rutherford Hayes served as President during what period in American history?

    A Progressive Era
    B Era of Good Feelings
    C Gilded Age
    D Antebellum Era

Q8 Workers in which industry went on a major strike in 1877?

    A Steel
    B Shipping
    C Railroad
    D Farming

Q9 How old was Rutherford Hayes when his father died?

    A Not yet born
    B 5
    C 19
    D 64

Q10 What famous Confederate raider did Rutherford Hayes help defeat in 1863?

    A Joseph Shelby
    B William Quantrill
    C John Hunt Morgan
    D J.E.B. Stuart

Rutherford Hayes 2 (average)

Q1 How many terms did Rutherford Hayes serve as President?

Q2 What political party was Rutherford Hayes a member of during his presidency?

Q3 What political office did Rutherford Hayes hold prior to becoming President?

Q4 What 1878 act did Rutherford Hayes unsuccessfully veto?

Q5 Who served as Rutherford Hayes's Vice President?

Q6 Where did Rutherford Hayes train as a lawyer?

Q7 Rutherford Hayes's son, James Webb Cook Hayes, was awarded the Congressional Medal of Honour for meritorious service in what country?

Q8 What rank did Rutherford Hayes reach in the United States Army?

Q9 Which President served as a private in Rutherford Hayes's regiment?

Q10 An elector from what northern state was disqualified during the 1876 presidential election?

Rutherford Hayes 3 (expert)

Q1 What nickname have historians given to Rutherford Hayes's wife?

Q2 What is the name of Rutherford Hayes's estate in Fremont, Ohio?

Q3 How many children did Rutherford Hayes have?

Q4 What regiment of the Ohio Volunteer Infantry did Hayes serve with during the American Civil War?

Q5 How old was Rutherford Hayes when he died?

Q6 Rutherford Hayes named one of his sons after which army officer?

Q7 Where did Rutherford Hayes's inauguration take place?

Q8 Who served as Rutherford Hayes's Secretary of State?

Q9 Villa Hayes, named in honour of Rutherford Hayes, is located in what country?

Q10 What 1873 act placed the USA firmly on the gold standard?

James Garfield 1 (easy)

Q1 Who served as James Garfield's Vice President?

    A Chester Arthur
    B Frederick Theodore Frelinghuysen
    C Charles Julius Guiteau
    D William Evarts

Q2 What position did James Gillespie Blaine hold in James Garfield's administration?

    A Secretary of War
    B Secretary of State
    C Ambassador to the United Kingdom
    D Secretary of the Treasury

Q3 What was James Garfield's middle name?

    A Seamus
    B Damien
    C Dillon
    D Abram

Q4 How long did James Garfield serve as President?

    A Under a year
    B 2 years
    C 4 years
    D 8 years

Q5 What was the name of James Garfield's wife?

    A Delilah
    B Lucretia
    C Daniela
    D Martha

Q6 What was James Garfield's nickname?

    A The Cat
    B Old Warhorse
    C Preacher President
    D The Corrupt Bargainer

Q7 James Garfield served as a Major General in what war?

    A Mexican-American War
    B Spanish-American War
    C American Civil War
    D War of 1812

Q8 What political office did James Garfield occupy before becoming President?

    A Senator
    B State Governor
    C Congressman
    D Supreme Court Justice

Q9 Which famous inventor tried to find the bullet in James Garfield using a metal detector?

    A Thomas Edison
    B Alexander Graham Bell
    C Eli Whitney
    D Wernher von Braun

Q10 Where was James Garfield born?

    A In a field
    B In a log cabin
    C In a plantation house
    D On board a ship

James Garfield 2 (average)

Q1 How did James Garfield die?

Q2 What US state was James Garfield born in?

Q3 James Garfield was primarily raised by which relative?

Q4 James Garfield's son, James Rudolph Garfield, served on which President's cabinet?

Q5 What church was James Garfield a member of?

Q6 What college did Garfield graduate from in 1856?

Q7 Where was the 1880 Republican National Convention held?

Q8 Who was James Garfield's opponent in the 1880 presidential election?

Q9 Which judge did James Garfield successfully appoint to the Supreme Court?

Q10 In what US state did James Garfield die?

James Garfield 3 (expert)

Q1 What is Charles Julius Guiteau known for?

Q2 The James Garfield Memorial is situated in what cemetery?

Q3 James Garfield went to what railway station shortly before his death?

Q4 In what year did James Garfield allegedly have an extramarital affair?

Q5 What Ohio district did James Garfield represent in Congress?

Q6 What rival of James Garfield protested several of his appointments as President?

Q7 Which three key battles did James Garfield participate in?

Q8 On which ballot did James Garfield secure the Republican nomination for President?

Q9 What position did James Garfield appoint William Henry Robertson to in 1881?

Q10 After leaving home at the age of 16, what did James Garfield find work on?

Chester Arthur 1 (easy)

Q1 What was Chester Arthur's middle name?

   A Andrew
   B Adam
   C Alan
   D Arnold

Q2 What political office did Chester Arthur occupy before becoming President?

   A Governor of Iowa
   B Speaker of the House of Representatives
   C Vice President
   D Attorney General

Q3 What political party was Chester Arthur a member of during his presidency?

   A Republican
   B Libertarian
   C Democratic
   D Constitutional Union

Q4 What US state was Chester Arthur born in?

   A Vermont
   B California
   C New York
   D Maine

Q5 How was the First Lady – Mary Arthur McElroy – during Chester Arthur's presidency related to him?

   A Sister
   B Wife
   C Daughter
   D Cousin

Q6 In what city did Chester Arthur's inauguration take place?

    A Baltimore
    B Washington D.C.
    C Chicago
    D New York

Q7 In what present-day country was Chester Arthur's father born?

    A USA
    B Northern Ireland
    C Germany
    D Sweden

Q8 Chester Arthur suffered from Bright's Disease, which affected what part of his body?

    A Heart
    B Lungs
    C Kidneys
    D Brain

Q9 How many children did Chester Arthur have?

    A 0
    B 3
    C 7
    D 10

Q10 Who served as Secretary of State during Chester Arthur's presidency?

    A John Nelson
    B Lewis Cass
    C Jeremiah Black
    D Frederick Theodore Frelinghuysen

Chester Arthur 2 (average)

Q1 What was the name of Chester Arthur's wife?

Q2 Who served as Vice President during Chester Arthur's presidency?

Q3 Who defeated Chester Arthur at the 1884 Republican National Convention?

Q4 What college did Chester Arthur graduate from in 1848?

Q5 What US state did Chester Arthur move to during his childhood?

Q6 Who was the Pendleton Civil Service Reform Act named after?

Q7 What rank did Chester Arthur hold during the American Civil War?

Q8 How many terms did Chester Arthur serve as President?

Q9 The Supreme Court ruled parts of what act unconstitutional in the *Civil Rights Cases* (1883)?

Q10 Who served as Secretary of the Navy for the majority of Chester Arthur's presidency?

Chester Arthur 3 (expert)

Q1 Who swore Chester Arthur into office?

Q2 In what year was the Pendleton Civil Service Reform Act passed?

Q3 Chester Arthur is buried in what cemetery?

Q4 In what year was the Chinese Exclusion Act passed?

Q5 Whose law firm did Chester Arthur join in 1854?

Q6 Rutherford B. Hayes fired Chester Arthur from what position in 1878?

Q7 How many judges did Chester Arthur successfully appoint to the Supreme Court?

Q8 Chester Arthur was closely associated with which New York Senator?

Q9 The nickname 'Bourbon Democrat' (referring to more conservative members of the Democratic Party) derived from what country's monarchy?

Q10 How many states were admitted to the Union during Chester Arthur's presidency?

Grover Cleveland 1 (easy)

Q1 Grover Cleveland is the only President to do what?

    A Perform in a circus
    B Marry three times
    C Serve non-consecutive terms
    D Travel to all seven continents

Q2 What political party was Grover Cleveland a member of during his presidency?

    A Republican
    B Democratic
    C Free Soil
    D Constitutional Union

Q3 What US state was Grover Cleveland born in?

    A New Hampshire
    B New York
    C New Jersey
    D Vermont

Q4 Who served as Grover Cleveland's first First Lady?

    A Frances Folsom Cleveland Preston
    B Ann Neal
    C Rose Cleveland
    D Philippa Foot

Q5 How many people served as Vice President under Grover Cleveland?

    A 0
    B 1
    C 2
    D 3

Q6 Who did Grover Cleveland defeat in the 1884 presidential election?

A Chester Arthur
B James Gillespie Blaine
C Benjamin Harrison
D William Pierce Frye

Q7 Grover Cleveland served as Mayor of what city?

A Newark
B Manchester
C Concord
D Buffalo

Q8 Grover Cleveland won the popular vote in how many presidential elections?

A 0
B 1
C 2
D 3

Q9 What was Grover Cleveland's father's occupation?

A Presbyterian minister
B Congressman
C Shoemaker
D Journalist

Q10 The Murchison letter was a scandal involving what country's ambassador to the USA?

A France
B United Kingdom
C Australia
D Cyprus

Grover Cleveland 2 (average)

Q1 In what city did Thomas Hendricks die?

Q2 Grover Cleveland occupied what political office before becoming President?

Q3 The Pullman Strike involved workers from which sector?

Q4 Grover Cleveland was trained in what occupation?

Q5 What was the name of Grover Cleveland's estate in Bourne, Massachusetts?

Q6 Coxey's Army marched on what city?

Q7 What territory did the USA acquire during Grover Cleveland's presidency?

Q8 The USA intervened in a dispute between the United Kingdom and what other country in 1895?

Q9 What illness did Grover Cleveland suffer from in 1893?

Q10 What state was admitted to the Union in 1896?

Grover Cleveland 3 (expert)

Q1 In what year did Grover Cleveland marry Frances Folsom Cleveland Preston?

Q2 In what year of Grover Cleveland's presidency did a serious economic depression occur?

Q3 What was Grover Cleveland's daughter, Ruth Cleveland, popularly known as?

Q4 What name was given to Republicans who supported Grover Cleveland in the 1884 presidential election?

Q5 What party system ended during Grover Cleveland's presidency?

Q6 How many justices did Grover Cleveland successfully appoint to the Supreme Court?

Q7 The Wilson–Gorman Tariff Act reduced rates set in what 1890 tariff?

Q8 The Enabling Act of 1889 allowed which 4 states to be admitted to the Union?

Q9 What did Grover Cleveland die from?

Q10 How many people served as Secretary of State under Grover Cleveland?

Benjamin Harrison 1 (easy)

Q1 Benjamin Harrison was unsuccessful in his bid to become Governor of what US state?

    A Ohio
    B Indiana
    C Michigan
    D Minnesota

Q2 What relation was the Founding Father, Benjamin Harrison V, to Benjamin Harrison?

    A Great uncle
    B Second cousin
    C Grandfather
    D Great grandfather

Q3 What political party was Benjamin Harrison a member of during his presidency?

    A Republican
    B Democratic
    C Libertarian
    D Socialist

Q4 Who did Benjamin Harrison defeat in the 1888 presidential election?

    A William McKinley
    B Grover Cleveland
    C Theodore Roosevelt
    D John Sherman

Q5 How many times did Benjamin Harrison get married?

    A 0
    B 1
    C 2
    D 3

Q6 What US state was Benjamin Harrison born in?

A Ohio
B Indiana
C New Jersey
D Kansas

Q7 What relation was Mary Harrison McKee to Benjamin Harrison?

A Sister
B Aunt
C Cousin
D Daughter

Q8 How many states were admitted to the Union during Benjamin Harrison's presidency?

A 0
B 1
C 2
D 6

Q9 What caused Benjamin Harrison's death?

A Influenza
B Heart attack
C Smallpox
D Cancer

Q10 What university did Benjamin Harrison graduate from in 1852?

A Ohio State University
B Oklahoma State University
C Princeton University
D Miami University

Benjamin Harrison 2 (average)

Q1 How many terms did Benjamin Harrison serve as President?

Q2 Who served as Vice President during Benjamin Harrison's presidency?

Q3 Which President was Benjamin Harrison's grandfather?

Q4 Besides from being a politician, what was Benjamin Harrison's occupation?

Q5 Which President did Benjamin Harrison appoint to the United States Court of Appeals for the Sixth Circuit?

Q6 The Benjamin Harrison Presidential Site is located in what city?

Q7 What political position did Benjamin Harrison's father hold?

Q8 Benjamin Harrison turned down an offer to serve on which President's cabinet?

Q9 In what city was the 1888 Republican National Convention held?

Q10 What country did Benjamin Harrison represent before an international arbitration panel in Paris?

Benjamin Harrison 3 (expert)

Q1 In what presidential election was Benjamin Harrison defeated by Grover Cleveland?

Q2 What tariff was passed in 1890?

Q3 In what year was the Sherman Antitrust Act passed?

Q4 What infantry regiment was Benjamin Harrison in during the American Civil War?

Q5 The body of Benjamin Harrison's father was stolen by grave robbers and sold to a university in what city?

Q6 How many justices did Benjamin Harrison successfully appoint to the Supreme Court?

Q7 Who died during Benjamin Harrison's 1892 re-election campaign?

Q8 James Baird Weaver was what political party's candidate in the 1892 presidential election?

Q9 The *Baltimore* crisis was a diplomatic incident between the USA and what other country?

Q10 Created in 1891, what was the USA's first national forest?

William McKinley 1 (easy)

Q1 In what city was William McKinley assassinated?

    A Charleston
    B Philadelphia
    C Chicago
    D Buffalo

Q2 Who was William McKinley's first Vice President?

    A Theodore Roosevelt
    B Garret Hobart
    C James Campbell
    D Woodrow Wilson

Q3 William McKinley was born in what US state?

    A New York
    B Ohio
    C Texas
    D Arkansas

Q4 How was William McKinley's assassin executed?

    A Electric chair
    B Hung
    C Firing squad
    D Lethal injection

Q5 What was the name of William McKinley's wife?

    A Martine
    B Dina
    C Ida
    D Eva

Q6 William McKinley was the last President to have served in what war?

    A War of 1812
    B Mexican-American War
    C Spanish-American War
    D American Civil War

Q7 Who did William McKinley defeat in the 1896 presidential election?

    A Woodrow Wilson
    B Robert Lansing
    C Grover Cleveland
    D William Jennings Bryan

Q8 What war did the USA participate in during William McKinley's presidency?

    A Spanish-American War
    B First World War
    C Mexican-American War
    D Russian Civil War

Q9 What rank did William McKinley reach in the army?

    A Captain
    B Colonel
    C Major
    D Brigadier General

Q10 What church was William McKinley a member of?

    A Anglican
    B Presbyterian
    C Methodist
    D Catholic

William McKinley 2 (average)

Q1 Who assassinated William McKinley?

Q2 How many times was William McKinley elected President?

Q3 What political office did William McKinley occupy before becoming President?

Q4 Who swore William McKinley into office as President?

Q5 How many states were admitted to the Union during William McKinley's presidency?

Q6 Besides from being a politician, what was William McKinley's occupation?

Q7 Who delivered the Cross of Gold speech in 1896?

Q8 What political position did William McKinley hold when the McKinley Tariff was passed?

Q9 What cabinet-level position was John Milton Hay appointed to by William McKinley in 1898?

Q10 Which US Navy ship was sunk in Havana Harbour in 1898?

William McKinley 3 (expert)

Q1 What event was William McKinley attending when he was assassinated?

Q2 In what year did the USA acquire Puerto Rico and Guam?

Q3 Where was the treaty signed that ended the Spanish-American War?

Q4 Which Ohio Senator was a close friend and political ally of William McKinley?

Q5 In what year was the Gold Standard Act passed?

Q6 Which infantry regiment did William McKinley serve in?

Q7 In what year did William McKinley offer rioting miners legal representation *pro bono*?

Q8 How many individuals served as Secretary of State under William McKinley?

Q9 What type of Democrats opposed William Jennings Bryan?

Q10 The First and Second Open Door Note concerned what country?

Theodore Roosevelt 1 (easy)

Q1 What city was Theodore Roosevelt born in?

A Boston
B Louisville
C New York City
D Hartford

Q2 What political position did Theodore Roosevelt hold before becoming President?

A Congressman
B Senator
C Vice President
D None

Q3 In what era of American history did Theodore Roosevelt serve as President?

A Progressive Era
B Gilded Age
C Era of Good Feelings
D Depression

Q4 What political party was Theodore Roosevelt a member of during his presidency?

A Democratic
B Republican
C Libertarian
D Whig

Q5 How many times did Theodore Roosevelt marry?

A 0
B 1
C 2
D 5

Q6 Theodore Roosevelt served as Governor of what US state?

    A Kentucky
    B Connecticut
    C Massachusetts
    D New York

Q7 After the 1912 presidential election, Theodore Roosevelt embarked on a scientific expedition in what country?

    A Mexico
    B Sudan
    C Brazil
    D Japan

Q8 How many new national parks did Theodore Roosevelt establish during his presidency?

    A 0
    B 1
    C 5
    D 9

Q9 What nickname was given to the 1st United States Volunteer Cavalry?

    A Roosevelt's Men
    B Rough Riders
    C Phantoms of the Highway
    D Teddy's Boys

Q10 What war did Theodore Roosevelt participate in?

    A First World War
    B Mexican-American War
    C Spanish-American War
    D American Civil War

Theodore Roosevelt 2 (average)

Q1 Who swore Theodore Roosevelt in as President after the death of William McKinley?

Q2 Who was Theodore Roosevelt's opponent in the 1904 presidential election?

Q3 What political party was Theodore Roosevelt a candidate for in the 1912 presidential election?

Q4 Who served as First Lady during Theodore Roosevelt's presidency?

Q5 Who served as Vice President during Theodore Roosevelt's presidency?

Q6 What military award did Theodore Roosevelt posthumously receive?

Q7 What Central American canal began construction during Theodore Roosevelt's presidency?

Q8 Theodore Roosevelt was well-known for saying 'Speak softly and carry a...' what?

Q9 What was the name of Theodore Roosevelt's addition to the Monroe Doctrine?

Q10 The Hay–Bunau-Varilla Treaty was a treaty between the USA and what other country?

Theodore Roosevelt 3 (expert)

Q1 In what house was Theodore Roosevelt sworn in as President in 1901?

Q2 What did Alice Hathaway Roosevelt die from?

Q3 What book by Theodore Roosevelt was published in 1882?

Q4 What was the name of the residence Theodore Roosevelt owned near Oyster Bay?

Q5 Abram Hewitt defeated Theodore Roosevelt in an 1886 election to become what?

Q6 Which two close relatives of Theodore Roosevelt died on 14th February 1884?

Q7 During his time at university, what newspaper did Theodore Roosevelt serve as the editor for?

Q8 Who was Theodore Roosevelt's Secretary of War between 1904 and 1908?

Q9 What war did Theodore Roosevelt mediate an end to in 1905?

Q10 What was the name of Theodore Roosevelt's domestic programme?

William Howard Taft 1 (easy)

Q1 Who served as William Howard Taft's Vice President?

  A Woodrow Wilson
  B James Sherman
  C Charles Hughes
  D Warren Harding

Q2 What city was William Howard Taft born in?

  A Cincinnati
  B New York
  C New Orleans
  D St Louis

Q3 What was the name of William Howard Taft's wife?

  A Beverley
  B Diana
  C Margaret
  D Helen

Q4 Eugene Victor Debs represented which political party in five presidential elections?

  A Democratic
  B Republican
  C Progressive
  D Socialist

Q5 What political position did William Howard Taft hold during the 1920s?

  A President
  B Senate Minority Leader
  C Chief Justice of the Supreme Court
  D None

Q6 What cabinet position did William Howard Taft hold in Theodore Roosevelt's administration?

  A Secretary of War
  B Attorney General
  C Vice President
  D Secretary of State

Q7 What university did William Howard Taft graduate from in 1878?

  A Princeton University
  B Yale University
  C Harvard University
  D George Mason University

Q8 Which President appointed William Howard Taft as Governor-General of the Philippines?

  A William McKinley
  B Grover Cleveland
  C Benjamin Harrison
  D Theodore Roosevelt

Q9 William Howard Taft was trained in what profession?

  A Engineer
  B Architect
  C Diplomat
  D Lawyer

Q10 How many Associate Justices did William Howard Taft successfully appoint to the Supreme Court?

  A 0
  B 1
  C 2
  D 5

William Howard Taft 2 (average)

Q1 How many terms did William Howard Taft serve as President?

Q2 What political party was William Howard Taft a member of during his presidency?

Q3 Who served as William Howard Taft's Secretary of State?

Q4 Who did William Howard Taft defeat in the 1908 presidential election?

Q5 What was the name of William Howard Taft's father?

Q6 The William Howard Taft National Historic Site is located in what US state?

Q7 Carrie Nation was a radical member of what movement?

Q8 Who swore in William Howard Taft as President?

Q9 After becoming President, William Howard Taft kept Jim Wilson in what cabinet position?

Q10 The United States occupation of Nicaragua was part of what series of interventions by the US government in Central America?

William Howard Taft 3 (expert)

Q1 Who were the four main candidates in the 1912 presidential election?

Q2 What two states were admitted to the Union during William Howard Taft's presidency?

Q3 In what cemetery is William Howard Taft buried?

Q4 Both William Howard Taft and his father were members of what student society?

Q5 The Pinchot–Ballinger controversy was a dispute between the U.S. Forest Service Chief, Gifford Pinchot, and who?

Q6 Who did William Howard Taft successfully appoint as Chief Justice of the Supreme Court?

Q7 In what year was the Sixteenth Amendment to the United States Constitution ratified?

Q8 What controversial tariff was passed early in William Howard Taft's presidency?

Q9 What was William Howard Taft's foreign policy strategy in Latin America and East Asia referred to as?

Q10 How many children did William Howard Taft have?

Woodrow Wilson 1 (easy)

Q1 What war was the USA involved in during Woodrow Wilson's presidency?

    A Korean War
    B American Civil War
    C Spanish-American War
    D First World War

Q2 Woodrow Wilson served as President of what university?

    A Brown University
    B Princeton University
    C Harvard University
    D Yale University

Q3 Who served as Vice President during Woodrow Wilson's presidency?

    A Frank Hall
    B Thomas Riley Marshall
    C Franklin Delano Roosevelt
    D William Jennings Bryan

Q4 What US state was Woodrow Wilson born in?

    A Virginia
    B Alabama
    C North Carolina
    D Indiana

Q5 What international organisation preceded the United Nations?

    A Council of States
    B Paris Accords
    C International Peace Committee
    D League of Nations

Q6 Which amendment to the United States Constitution abolished alcohol?

    A 16th
    B 17th
    C 18th
    D 19th

Q7 Woodrow Wilson served as Governor of what US state before becoming President?

    A New York
    B New Jersey
    C Georgia
    D Virginia

Q8 How many individuals served as First Lady during Woodrow Wilson's presidency?

    A 0
    B 1
    C 2
    D 3

Q9 How was Margaret Woodrow Wilson related to Woodrow Wilson?

    A Daughter
    B Sister
    C Mother
    D Aunt

Q10 Ellen Axson Wilson's death was related to what organ?

    A Brain
    B Lungs
    C Kidneys
    D Liver

Woodrow Wilson 2 (average)

Q1 What political party was Woodrow Wilson a member of during his presidency?

Q2 How many terms did Woodrow Wilson serve as President?

Q3 Who did Woodrow Wilson beat in the 1916 presidential election?

Q4 What term was used to refer to Woodrow Wilson's foreign policy?

Q5 What was the name of Woodrow Wilson's principals for peace, which he hoped would bring an end to the First World War?

Q6 Woodrow Wilson served as President during what era of American history?

Q7 The Zimmermann Telegram proposed an alliance between what two countries?

Q8 What university did Woodrow Wilson receive his PhD from?

Q9 The New Freedom was Woodrow Wilson's campaign platform in what presidential election?

Q10 What side did Woodrow Wilson's family support during the American Civil War?

Woodrow Wilson 3 (expert)

Q1 In what year was the Revenue Act passed?

Q2 In what year was the Federal Reserve System created?

Q3 What did Woodrow Wilson suffer from in 1919?

Q4 What did Woodrow Wilson do to try to rally public support for the League of Nations?

Q5 What fraternity was Woodrow Wilson a member of?

Q6 What major labour uprising ended in 1914?

Q7 What 1917 act granted greater autonomy to Puerto Rico?

Q8 What act authorised the federal government to raise a national army for service in World War I through conscription?

Q9 Who were the Big Four at the 1919 Paris Peace Conference?

Q10 With regards to the Treaty of Versailles and the League of Nations, who led the 'Reservationists' in Congress?

Warren Harding 1 (easy)

Q1 What was Warren Harding's middle name?

    A Ryan
    B Jordan
    C Gamaliel
    D Alphonso

Q2 In what city did Warren Harding die?

    A San Francisco
    B New York
    C Washington D.C.
    D Oklahoma City

Q3 What was Warren Harding's wife called?

    A Abigail
    B Florence
    C Jana
    D Siena

Q4 What political party was Warren Harding a member of during his presidency?

    A Republican
    B Democratic
    C Whig
    D Progressive

Q5 What political position did Warren Harding hold before becoming President?

    A Associate Justice of the Supreme Court
    B Congressman
    C Senator
    D Vice President

Q6 Who did Warren Harding face in the 1920 presidential election?

    A James Middleton Cox
    B William Jennings Bryan
    C Henry Cabot Lodge
    D Earl Bloom

Q7 What was Teapot Dome?

    A Warren Harding's home
    B A political scandal
    C A proposed free trade organisation
    D The place where Warren Harding died

Q8 'Return to…' what was used as a campaign slogan by Warren Harding during the 1920 presidential election?

    A Greatness
    B Normalcy
    C Our roots
    D Prosperity

Q9 How was Nan Britton associated with Warren Harding?

    A Secretary
    B Mistress
    C Favourite singer
    D Business partners

Q10 What political position did Charles Evans Hughes hold during Warren Harding's presidency?

    A Secretary of State
    B Attorney General
    C Secretary of Commerce
    D Secretary of War

Warren Harding 2 (average)

Q1 What US state was Warren Harding born in?

Q2 Who served as Vice President during Warren Harding's presidency?

Q3 In what city was the Republican National Convention held?

Q4 In what years did Warren Harding serve as President?

Q5 What relation was Elizabeth Ann Blaesing to Warren Harding?

Q6 How many terms did Warren Harding serve as President?

Q7 What position did Herbert Hoover hold in Warren Harding's cabinet?

Q8 Who swore Warren Harding into office as President?

Q9 Who did Warren Harding appoint as Chief Justice of the Supreme Court?

Q10 What did Warren Harding die from?

Warren Harding 3 (expert)

Q1 What newspaper did Warren Harding own?

Q2 Warren Harding clinched the 1920 Republican nomination for President on what ballot?

Q3 How many Supreme Court Justices did Warren Harding successfully appoint during his presidency?

Q4 How many countries signed the Washington Naval Treaty?

Q5 What college did Warren Harding attend?

Q6 During his presidential election campaign, Warren Harding's opponents spread rumours that some of Harding's ancestors were what?

Q7 The Knox–Porter Resolution officially ended the USA's involvement in what?

Q8 In what year of Warren Harding's presidency did an economic depression end?

Q9 In what year was the Fordney–McCumber Tariff passed?

Q10 What was the name of the major railroad strike that occurred during Warren Harding's presidency?

Calvin Coolidge 1 (easy)

Q1 According to Calvin Coolidge 'the chief business of the American people is...' what?

    A Farming
    B Banking
    C Business
    D Building

Q2 What political position did Calvin Coolidge hold before becoming President?

    A Senate Minority Leader
    B Vice President
    C Chief Justice of the Supreme Court
    D Attorney General

Q3 The Calvin Coolidge House is located in what US state?

    A Vermont
    B Connecticut
    C Massachusetts
    D Illinois

Q4 Calvin Coolidge's son, Calvin Coolidge Junior, died after playing what sport without socks?

    A Tennis
    B Baseball
    C American Football
    D Ice Hockey

Q5 What was the name of Calvin Coolidge's wife?

    A Grace
    B Eda
    C Rose
    D Wendy

Q6 What term is used to refer to the 1920s?

A Peaceful Twenties
B Terrible Twenties
C Roaring Twenties
D Turbulent Twenties

Q7 Which of the following was Calvin Coolidge's childhood home?

A Tranquil Cottage
B Merry Loge
C Calvin's Castle
D Coolidge Homestead

Q8 On how many occasions was Calvin Coolidge elected President?

A 0
B 1
C 2
D 3

Q9 Which relative of Calvin Coolidge administered his presidential oath of office in 1923?

A Brother
B Father
C Uncle
D Cousin

Q10 Up to how many hours a day did Calvin Coolidge spend sleeping?

A 4
B 6
C 8
D 15

Calvin Coolidge 2 (average)

Q1 In what US state was Calvin Coolidge born?

Q2 What political party was Calvin Coolidge a member of during his presidency?

Q3 Who served as Vice President during Calvin Coolidge's presidency?

Q4 Calvin Coolidge's response to what 1919 strike thrust him into the national spotlight?

Q5 In what building did Calvin Coolidge's 1923 inauguration take place?

Q6 What college did Calvin Coolidge attend?

Q7 Calvin Coolidge served as Governor of what US state?

Q8 What was Calvin Coolidge's nickname?

Q9 Calvin Coolidge was born on what American holiday?

Q10 What major river flooded in 1927?

Calvin Coolidge 3 (expert)

Q1 What two opponents did Calvin Coolidge face in the 1924 presidential election?

Q2 What fraternity was Calvin Coolidge a member of?

Q3 In what cemetery is Calvin Coolidge buried?

Q4 Which of Calvin Coolidge's children died in 2000?

Q5 What controversial plan to subsidise American agriculture by raising the domestic prices of farm products did Calvin Coolidge veto?

Q6 How many individuals served as Secretary of State during Calvin Coolidge's presidency?

Q7 In what year was the Indian Citizenship Act passed?

Q8 Prior to the 1928 presidential election, Calvin Coolidge handed out strips of paper to members of the press saying what?

Q9 In what year did Calvin Coolidge leave office as President?

Q10 What was constitutionally banned during Calvin Coolidge's presidency?

Herbert Hoover 1 (easy)

Q1 Who did Herbert Hoover defeat in the 1928 presidential election?

    A Franklin Roosevelt
    B Al Smith
    C Harry Truman
    D Thomas Marshall

Q2 Who served as Vice President during Herbert Hoover's presidency?

    A Charles Gates Dawes
    B Charles Evans Hughes
    C Dwight Eisenhower
    D Charles Curtis

Q3 Herbert Hoover was born in what US state?

    A New Hampshire
    B New Jersey
    C Illinois
    D Iowa

Q4 Herbert Hoover held what position on Calvin Coolidge's cabinet?

    A Secretary of Commerce
    B Secretary of State
    C Secretary of Agriculture
    D Secretary of War

Q5 What was the name of Herbert Hoover's wife?

    A Lou
    B Marnie
    C Danielle
    D Una

Q6 Herbert Hoover led the Commission for Relief in what country?

A Spain
B Austria
C Belgium
D Germany

Q7 What religious group was Herbert Hoover's family a part of?

A Puritan
B Mormon
C Quaker
D Jehovah's Witnesses

Q8 What university did Herbert Hoover graduate from in 1895?

A Ohio State University
B Stanford University
C Oklahoma State University
D Yale University

Q9 What relation was Herbert Hoover sent to live with in 1885?

A Father
B Uncle
C Grandmother
D Second cousin

Q10 What sector did Herbert Hoover work in after graduating from university?

A Journalism
B Construction
C Mining
D Law

Herbert Hoover 2 (average)

Q1 Herbert Hoover was a member of what political party during his presidency?

Q2 In what presidential election did Franklin Roosevelt defeat Herbert Hoover?

Q3 What disaster occurred at the start of Herbert Hoover's presidency?

Q4 Who swore Herbert Hoover in as President?

Q5 What rebellion broke out while Herbert Hoover was working in China?

Q6 What protectionist tariff was passed by Herbert Hoover's administration in 1930?

Q7 Herbert Hoover refused to abandon what monetary system?

Q8 What position did Henry Lewis Stimson hold on Herbert Hoover's cabinet?

Q9 What group marched on Washington D.C. in July 1932?

Q10 What dictator did Herbert Hoover meet in 1938?

Herbert Hoover 3 (expert)

Q1 In what year was the Hoover Dam opened?

Q2 In what city was the 1928 Republican National Convention held?

Q3 In what year did Herbert Hoover die?

Q4 What subject did Herbert Hoover study at university?

Q5 How many children did Herbert Hoover have?

Q6 In what year was the Agricultural Marketing Act passed?

Q7 What name was given to the shanty towns built during the Great Depression by the homeless?

Q8 Which anarchist attempted to blow up Henry Hoover's train while he was visiting South America?

Q9 In what year was the Hoover Moratorium made?

Q10 What party system came to an end during Herbert Hoover's presidency?

Franklin Roosevelt 1 (easy)

Q1 What was Franklin Roosevelt's middle name?

   A James
   B Tyson
   C Harrison
   D Delano

Q2 How many presidential elections did Franklin Roosevelt win?

   A 0
   B 1
   C 2
   D 4

Q3 Franklin Roosevelt became President during what crisis?

   A First World War
   B Great Depression
   C Secession of southern states
   D Watergate scandal

Q4 What was the name of Franklin Roosevelt's domestic economic programme?

   A Recover and Revive
   B Basic Need
   C New Deal
   D Great Society

Q5 What was the name of Franklin Roosevelt's wife?

   A Anne
   B Beatrice
   C Eleanor
   D Sibyl

Q6 In what US state was Franklin Roosevelt born?

    A New Jersey
    B New York
    C Washington
    D Oregon

Q7 What political position did Franklin Roosevelt hold immediately prior to becoming President?

    A Secretary of State
    B Congressman
    C Senator
    D State Governor

Q8 Franklin Roosevelt was whose running mate in the 1920 presidential election?

    A Woodrow Wilson
    B Warren Harding
    C James Cox
    D William Jennings Bryan

Q9 In what year did Franklin Roosevelt die?

    A 1939
    B 1945
    C 1947
    D 1958

Q10 What kind of illness did Franklin Roosevelt suffer from?

    A Malaria
    B Paralytic
    C Mental
    D Cancer

Franklin Roosevelt 2 (average)

Q1 What political party was Franklin Roosevelt a member of during his presidency?

Q2 How many individuals served as Vice President during Franklin Roosevelt's presidency?

Q3 What estate owned by Franklin Roosevelt was located in the town of Hyde Park?

Q4 Franklin Roosevelt was Assistant Secretary of what from 1913 to 1920?

Q5 What event caused the USA to enter the Second World War?

Q6 What were the fireside chats?

Q7 Franklin Roosevelt once said 'The only thing we have to fear is…' what?

Q8 What was Camp David called during Franklin Roosevelt's presidency?

Q9 Lend-Lease was a policy aimed at helping the Allied powers defeat what three countries during the Second World War?

Q10 In what year did Franklin Roosevelt deliver the Infamy Speech?

Franklin Roosevelt 3 (expert)

Q1 How were Theodore Roosevelt and Franklin Roosevelt related?

Q2 Who was the first female member of the US government's cabinet?

Q3 Who did Franklin Roosevelt famously have an affair with during the First World War?

Q4 In what house did Franklin Roosevelt die?

Q5 What amendment repealed the Eighteenth Amendment to the United States Constitution?

Q6 Who did Franklin Roosevelt defeat in the 1936 presidential election?

Q7 The Judicial Procedures Reform Bill of 1937 proposed to do what to the Supreme Court?

Q8 In what year was the Social Security Act passed?

Q9 Who served as Franklin Roosevelt's Secretary of Commerce between 1938 and 1940?

Q10 Formed in 1935, what did the acronym WPA stand for?

Harry Truman 1 (easy)

Q1 What US state was Harry Truman born in?

    A Maryland
    B Arkansas
    C Kentucky
    D Missouri

Q2 What was the name of Harry Truman's wife?

    A Dorothy
    B Elizabeth
    C Janet
    D Violet

Q3 In what year did Harry Truman become Vice President?

    A 1933
    B 1940
    C 1945
    D 1947

Q4 The Quebec Agreement was an agreement between the USA and what other country?

    A Canada
    B Soviet Union
    C China
    D United Kingdom

Q5 What political position did Harry Truman hold between 1935 and 1945?

    A State Governor
    B Mayor
    C Congressman
    D Senator

Q6 The Truman Committee was formed during what war?

    A Spanish-American War
    B First World War
    C Second World War
    D Cold War

Q7 What war took place between 1950 and 1953?

    A Korean War
    B Vietnam War
    C Banana Wars
    D Soviet-Afghan War

Q8 How many times was Harry Truman elected President?

    A 0
    B 1
    C 2
    D 3

Q9 What prolonged war began during Harry Truman's presidency?

    A War on Terror
    B American Indian Wars
    C Hundred Years' War
    D Cold War

Q10 In what US state did the first nuclear detonation take place?

    A Arizona
    B Texas
    C New Mexico
    D Nevada

Harry Truman 2 (average)

Q1 What political party was Harry Truman a member of during his presidency?

Q2 Who served as Vice President during Harry Truman's presidency?

Q3 What American initiative provided aid to Europe after the Second World War?

Q4 What two Japanese cities were atomic bombs dropped on?

Q5 The Truman Doctrine was an American foreign policy aimed at countering the influence of what country?

Q6 The Harry S. Truman National Historic Site is located in what city?

Q7 What war did Harry Truman serve in?

Q8 What was the name of Harry Truman's only child?

Q9 Who served as Secretary of State between 1947 and 1949?

Q10 What series of military tribunals took place between 1945 and 1946?

Harry Truman 3 (expert)

Q1 What two rivals did Harry Truman defeat in the 1948 presidential election?

Q2 In what years did the Berlin Airlift take place?

Q3 What 1948 executive order abolished discrimination on the basis of race, colour, religion or national origin in the United States Armed Forces?

Q4 What law school did Harry Truman drop out of?

Q5 What was the code name of the first detonation of a nuclear weapon?

Q6 In what years of Harry Truman's presidency did a massive wave of labour strikes take place?

Q7 What was Charlie Ross's role in Harry Truman's administration?

Q8 In what city was the 1948 Democratic National Convention held?

Q9 Who did Harry Truman relieve from his duties as General of the Army in 1951?

Q10 An attempt was made to assassinate Harry Truman in November 1950 while he was staying in what house?

Dwight Eisenhower 1 (easy)

Q1 Operation Torch was an Allied invasion of part of what continent?

    A Africa
    B Asia
    C Europe
    D South America

Q2 What political party was Dwight Eisenhower a member of during his presidency?

    A States' Rights Democratic Party
    B Independent
    C Democratic
    D Republican

Q3 Who served as Dwight Eisenhower's Vice President?

    A Adlai Ewing Stevenson II
    B John Fitzgerald Kennedy
    C Richard Nixon
    D Arthur Tedder

Q4 What was the name of Dwight Eisenhower's wife?

    A Mary-Jane
    B Mildred
    C Minnie
    D Mamie

Q5 What political position did Dwight Eisenhower's son, John Eisenhower, hold?

    A Attorney General
    B Senator from Iowa
    C Ambassador to Belgium
    D Mayor of Miami, Florida

Q6 What US state was Dwight Eisenhower born in?

    A Oklahoma
    B Texas
    C Iowa
    D Kansas

Q7 What was Dwight Eisenhower's nickname?

    A The Nazinator
    B The General
    C Stonewall
    D Ike

Q8 What was Dwight Eisenhower's rank during the Second World War?

    A Brigadier General
    B Colonel
    C Major
    D General of the Army

Q9 What was Dwight Eisenhower's original first name?

    A David
    B Andrew
    C Lukas
    D Tony

Q10 Dwight Eisenhower badly injured his knee playing what sport?

    A American Football
    B Ice Hockey
    C Baseball
    D Tennis

Dwight Eisenhower 2 (average)

Q1 Who did Dwight Eisenhower defeat in the 1952 presidential election?

Q2 Who administered Dwight Eisenhower's oath of office during his first inauguration as President?

Q3 What military academy did Dwight Eisenhower attend?

Q4 The Eisenhower Doctrine concerned what geographical region?

Q5 What war did Dwight Eisenhower help negotiate an end to in 1953?

Q6 What relation to Dwight Eisenhower is Camp David named after?

Q7 Dwight Eisenhower served as President of what university?

Q8 Who served as Secretary of State for the majority of Dwight Eisenhower's presidency?

Q9 Who did Dwight Eisenhower successfully appoint as Chief Justice of the Supreme Court?

Q10 What name was given to Dwight Eisenhower's national security policy?

Dwight Eisenhower 3 (expert)

Q1 Between what years did Dwight Eisenhower serve as President?

Q2 How old was Doud Eisenhower when he died?

Q3 What two copies of the Bible did Dwight Eisenhower place his hand on during his first inauguration as President?

Q4 What was West Point's class of 1915 known as?

Q5 In what year did the Supreme Court case *Brown v. Board of Education* take place?

Q6 In what years did Dwight Eisenhower serve as Supreme Allied Commander Europe?

Q7 What golf club did Dwight Eisenhower join in 1948?

Q8 Dwight Eisenhower approved what invasion of Cuba at the end of his presidency?

Q9 Who served as a Senator from Wisconsin between 1947 and 1957?

Q10 Construction of the Interstate Highway System was authorised by what act?

John Kennedy 1 (easy)

Q1 What was John Kennedy's middle name?

    A Fitzgerald
    B Jonas
    C Lamar
    D Brian

Q2 What was the name of John Kennedy's brother, who was also assassinated?

    A Wayne
    B Raymond
    C Earl
    D Robert

Q3 In what city was John Kennedy assassinated?

    A Dallas
    B Houston
    C Chicago
    D San Francisco

Q4 John Kennedy served as a Senator from what US state?

    A Rhode Island
    B Massachusetts
    C Virginia
    D New York

Q5 What was John Kennedy's wife called?

    A Carol
    B Jacqueline
    C Tanya
    D Lucy

Q6 What position did Lyndon Johnson hold in John Kennedy's administration?

A Vice President
B Secretary of State
C Secretary of War
D None

Q7 In what war did John Kennedy see military action?

A First World War
B Second World War
C Korean War
D Vietnam War

Q8 In what month of 1962 did the Cuban Missile Crisis occur?

A January
B April
C July
D October

Q9 The term 'New Frontier' was used by John Kennedy during what speech?

A Peace speech
B Nomination speech
C Dying speech
D Inauguration speech

Q10 The 1960 presidential election was the first election where how many US states participated?

A 48
B 49
C 50
D 52

John Kennedy 2 (average)

Q1 What political party was John Kennedy a member of during his presidency?

Q2 Who is believed to have assassinated John Kennedy?

Q3 What university did John Kennedy graduate from in 1940?

Q4 Who was John Kennedy's opponent in the 1960 presidential election?

Q5 What political position did Dean Rusk hold during John Kennedy's presidency?

Q6 In what town is the John Fitzgerald Kennedy National Historic Site located?

Q7 John Kennedy was the first follower of what church to become President?

Q8 At the time of his inauguration, John Kennedy was the youngest person to serve as President, with the exception of who?

Q9 Operation Northwoods was a proposed operation against what country?

Q10 Who became the first person to journey into outer space in 1961?

John Kennedy 3 (expert)

Q1 On what date was John Kennedy assassinated?

Q2 In what year were the Peace Corps created?

Q3 After being shot, what hospital was John Kennedy taken to for emergency medical treatment?

Q4 Who were John Kennedy's parents?

Q5 What book did John Kennedy publish in 1956?

Q6 What unofficial name was given to the commission that was set up to investigate the assassination of John Kennedy?

Q7 What type of flame is lit at John Kennedy's memorial

Q8 How did John Kennedy's son, John F. Kennedy Jr., die?

Q9 What was the name of the Danish journalist John Kennedy had a romantic relationship with?

Q10 What was different about the 1960 presidential debates?

Lyndon Johnson 1 (easy)

Q1 Lyndon Johnson was a native of what US state?

    A Texas
    B Louisiana
    C Indiana
    D Iowa

Q2 What political party was Lyndon Johnson a member of during his presidency?

    A Democratic
    B Republican
    C Libertarian
    D Constitutional Union

Q3 What was Lyndon Johnson's middle name?

    A Brutus
    B Baines
    C Benjamin
    D Barry

Q4 What name was given to the set of domestic programmes Lyndon Johnson launched in 1964-65?

    A Big Society
    B Great Society
    C Free Society
    D Equal Society

Q5 What was the name of Lyndon Johnson's wife?

    A Claudia
    B Mary
    C Jane
    D Reena

Q6 What war took place during Lyndon Johnson's presidency?

    A Soviet-Afghan War
    B Second World War
    C Korean War
    D Vietnam War

Q7 Who served as Lyndon Johnson's Vice President?

    A Richard Nixon
    B Hubert Humphrey
    C Robert McNamara
    D Eugene McCarthy

Q8 What political position did Lyndon Johnson hold before becoming John Kennedy's Vice President?

    A Chief Justice of the Supreme Court
    B Senate Majority Leader
    C Secretary of Defence
    D Speaker of the House of Representatives

Q9 What unofficial name was given to legislation first introduced by Lyndon Johnson during his 1964 State of the Union address?

    A Ethnic Minorities Bill
    B Pragmatic Solution
    C War on Poverty
    D Revive the Nation

Q10 What branch of the armed forces did Lyndon Johnson serve in?

    A Army
    B Navy
    C Airforce
    D Marines

Lyndon Johnson 2 (average)

Q1 Who was Lyndon Johnson's opponent in the 1964 presidential election?

Q2 What town was the place of Lyndon Johnson's birth and death?

Q3 What was Lyndon Johnson's wife's nickname?

Q4 How many full terms did Lyndon Johnson serve as President?

Q5 What position did Robert McNamara hold in Lyndon Johnson's administration?

Q6 What US Navy ship was involved in the Gulf of Tonkin incident?

Q7 What was Lyndon Johnson's father called?

Q8 Lyndon Johnson served as the editor of the *University Star* newspaper at what university?

Q9 Who served as Lyndon Johnson's Secretary of State?

Q10 Who was President when Lyndon Johnson died?

Lyndon Johnson 3 (expert)

Q1 In what year was the Wilderness Act passed?

Q2 What place did Lyndon Johnson finish in the 1968 Democratic Party presidential primaries?

Q3 In what year was the Gulf of Tonkin Resolution passed?

Q4 Who was the Democratic candidate in the 1968 presidential election?

Q5 A famous protest march took place in 1965 from Selma, Alabama to where?

Q6 What corporation did the Public Broadcasting Act establish in 1967?

Q7 In what year was the Model Cities Program ended?

Q8 In what city was the 1964 Democratic National Convention held?

Q9 The Lyndon Baines Johnson Library and Museum is located on the grounds of what university?

Q10 What name is used to refer to the series of race riots that swept across the USA in 1967?

Richard Nixon 1 (easy)

Q1 What was Richard Nixon's middle name?

A Riley
B Gabriel
C Milhous
D Jamie

Q2 How many individuals served as Vice President during Richard Nixon's presidency?

A 0
B 1
C 2
D 3

Q3 Richard Nixon served as Vice President under what President?

A Harry Truman
B Dwight Eisenhower
C John Kennedy
D Lyndon Johnson

Q4 Although her real first name was Thelma, what other name was Richard Nixon's wife known by?

A Caroline
B Dianne
C Frankie
D Patricia

Q5 Richard Nixon served as a Senator from what US state?

A California
B Arizona
C Virginia
D New Jersey

Q6 What war did Richard Nixon serve in?

A Second World War
B Korean War
C Vietnam War
D Soviet-Afghan War

Q7 The Anti-Ballistic Missile Treaty was an agreement between the USA and what other country?

A United Kingdom
B Republic of China
C People's Republic of China
D Soviet Union

Q8 Operation Nickel Grass involved delivering supplies to what country?

A South Vietnam
B Israel
C Republic of China
D West Germany

Q9 In what year did Richard Nixon resign as President?

A 1971
B 1972
C 1974
D 1975

Q10 What was the first space mission to successfully put man on the Moon?

A Apollo 9
B Apollo 10
C Apollo 11
D Apollo 12

Richard Nixon 2 (average)

Q1 What political party was Richard Nixon a member of?

Q2 Which two opponents did Richard Nixon face during the 1968 presidential election?

Q3 Pat Brown defeated Richard Nixon to be re-elected as what in 1962?

Q4 What government agency was created in December 1970?

Q5 Who was Richard Nixon's running mate in the 1968 presidential election?

Q6 Richard Nixon's administration supported a coup in what Latin American country in 1973?

Q7 Who was Richard Nixon's opponent in the 1972 presidential election?

Q8 What scandal led to Richard Nixon's resignation as President?

Q9 Who did Richard Nixon successfully appoint as Chief Justice of the Supreme Court?

Q10 Who was Richard Nixon named after?

Richard Nixon 3 (expert)

Q1 What mansion near San Clemente, California was owned by Richard Nixon?

Q2 Which alleged Soviet spy's trial resulted in Richard Nixon being thrust into the national spotlight?

Q3 In what year did Richard Nixon visit China?

Q4 Richard Nixon began a War on what in 1971?

Q5 Where is the Richard Nixon Presidential Library and Museum located?

Q6 Who granted Richard Nixon a full and unconditional pardon?

Q7 Richard Nixon died shortly after suffering from what?

Q8 What university did Richard Nixon attend?

Q9 What military rank did Richard Nixon achieve?

Q10 Who served as Richard Nixon's first Secretary of State?

Gerald Ford 1 (easy)

Q1 How many times was Gerald Ford elected President?

    A 0
    B 1
    C 2
    D 3

Q2 Who served as Gerald Ford's Vice President?

    A Hubert Humphrey
    B Leslie Arends
    C Spiro Agnew
    D Nelson Rockefeller

Q3 What was Gerald Ford's middle name?

    A Rudolph
    B James
    C Harry
    D Gregory

Q4 Gerald Ford became Richard Nixon's Vice President under what amendment to the United States Constitution?

    A 13th
    B 15th
    C 22nd
    D 25th

Q5 What US state was Gerald Ford born in?

    A Michigan
    B South Dakota
    C Nebraska
    D Idaho

Q6 What branch of the armed forces did Gerald Ford serve in?

A Army
B Airforce
C Navy
D Marines

Q7 What was the name of Gerald Ford's wife?

A Anne
B Elizabeth
C Yvette
D Nadia

Q8 What was the name of Gerald Ford's stepfather?

A Tyson
B Alexander
C Gerald
D Benjamin

Q9 The USA's involvement in what war ended during Gerald Ford's presidency?

A Korean War
B Vietnam War
C Soviet-Afghan War
D Cold War

Q10 How many days did Gerald Ford serve as President?

A 212
B 895
C 1,999
D 2,223

Gerald Ford 2 (average)

Q1 What political party was Gerald Ford a member of during his presidency?

Q2 Who won the 1976 presidential election?

Q3 What relation was Leslie Lynch King Sr. to Gerald Ford?

Q4 What rank did Gerald Ford reach in the Boy Scouts of America?

Q5 What sport did Gerald Ford play at university?

Q6 What university did Gerald Ford graduate from in 1935?

Q7 Gerald Ford was appointed as a member of what commission in 1963?

Q8 What political position did Gerald Ford hold prior to becoming Vice President?

Q9 Who did Gerald Ford replace as Vice President?

Q10 On what peninsula were two United States Army officers killed in an axe murder incident?

Gerald Ford 3 (expert)

Q1 What address was Gerald Ford born at?

Q2 The Gerald R. Ford Presidential Museum is located near what city?

Q3 What name was Gerald Ford given when he was born?

Q4 What rank did Gerald Ford achieve in the armed forces?

Q5 In what year were the Helsinki Accords signed?

Q6 What fraternity was Gerald Ford a member of?

Q7 What type of dog was Gerald Ford's pet, Liberty?

Q8 An outbreak of what in 1976 resulted in a mass immunisation programme?

Q9 Gerald Ford was the target of how many assassination attempts during his presidency?

Q10 What was the name of the only judge Gerald Ford successfully appointed to the Supreme Court?

Jimmy Carter 1 (easy)

Q1 What US state was Jimmy Carter born in?

    A New York
    B South Carolina
    C Georgia
    D Arizona

Q2 What is Jimmy Carter's middle name?

    A Earl
    B Travis
    C Ethan
    D Marcus

Q3 What is the name of Jimmy Carter's wife?

    A Sandra
    B Hayley
    C Rosalynn
    D Daniela

Q4 What political position did Jimmy Carter hold between 1971 and 1975?

    A Senator
    B State Governor
    C Vice President
    D President

Q5 Who served as Vice President during Jimmy Carter's presidency?

    A George Wallace
    B Walter Mondale
    C Hubert Humphrey
    D Nelson Rockefeller

Q6 What branch of the armed forces did Jimmy Carter serve in?

A Army
B Airforce
C Navy
D Marines

Q7 How many Supreme Court Justices did Jimmy Carter successfully appoint during his presidency?

A 0
B 2
C 4
D 7

Q8 Shortly after becoming President, Jimmy Carter pardoned draft evaders from what war?

A First World War
B Second World War
C Korean War
D Vietnam War

Q9 A hostage crisis took place in what country during Jimmy Carter's presidency?

A Iran
B Iraq
C Syria
D Soviet Union

Q10 The Three Mile Island accident took place in what US state?

A Michigan
B Pennsylvania
C North Dakota
D New Jersey

Jimmy Carter 2 (average)

Q1 Who did Jimmy Carter defeat in the 1976 presidential election?

Q2 What political party was Jimmy Carter a member of during his presidency?

Q3 What was Jimmy Carter awarded in 2002?

Q4 The Camp David Accords was an agreement between what two countries?

Q5 Jimmy Carter's administration imposed a grain embargo on the Soviet Union in response to them invading what country?

Q6 What Olympic Games did the USA boycott?

Q7 What position did Cyrus Vance hold during Jimmy Carter's presidency?

Q8 The Torrijos–Carter Treaties concerned what canal?

Q9 How many rounds of Strategic Arms Limitation Talks took place between the USA and the Soviet Union?

Q10 Operation Eagle Claw was an attempt to end what?

Jimmy Carter 3 (expert)

Q1 What two cabinet-level departments were created during Jimmy Carter's presidency?

Q2 In what year was the Carter Center founded?

Q3 What academy did Jimmy Carter graduate from in 1946?

Q4 In what year of Jimmy Carter's presidency did an oil crisis occur?

Q5 The Carter Doctrine concerned what gulf?

Q6 Jimmy Carter faced a challenge from what member of the Kennedy family in the 1980 presidential primaries?

Q7 What game show did Jimmy Carter appear on in 1973?

Q8 In what year was the Airline Deregulation Act passed?

Q9 Jimmy Carter was the first President to make a state visit to what region?

Q10 What illness was Jimmy Carter diagnosed with in 2015?

Ronald Reagan 1 (easy)

Q1 What US state was Ronald Reagan born in?

    A Illinois
    B California
    C Oregon
    D New York

Q2 What political party was Ronald Reagan a member of during his presidency?

    A Democratic
    B Republican
    C Independent
    D Libertarian

Q3 Who served as First Lady during Ronald Reagan's presidency?

    A Jane Wyman
    B Maureen Reagan
    C Nancy Reagan
    D Nelle Wilson

Q4 Ronald Reagan served as Governor of what US state?

    A California
    B Oregon
    C Rhode Island
    D Florida

Q5 Who served as Ronald Reagan's Vice President?

    A James Danforth Quayle
    B Robert Hutchinson Finch
    C George Herbert Walker Bush
    D Spiro Theodore Agnew

Q6 What was Ronald Reagan's occupation prior to entering politics?

A Entrepreneur
B Architect
C Actor
D Lawyer

Q7 What name was given to the economic policies promoted by Ronald Reagan during his presidency?

A Reagan's Deal
B Fiscal Conservatism
C Reaganomics
D Regan's Plan

Q8 Who was Ronald Reagan shot and wounded by on 30th March 1981?

A James Earl Ray
B John Hinckley Jr.
C Charles Wilkes Booth
D Lee Harvey Oswald

Q9 Where did Ronald Reagan say 'Tear down this wall!' in a speech?

A West Berlin
B Washington D.C.
C Durham
D Moscow

Q10 What branch of the military did Ronald Reagan serve in?

A Army
B Air Force
C Navy
D Marines

Ronald Reagan 2 (average)

Q1 Who did Ronald Reagan divorce?

Q2 Who did Ronald Reagan beat in the 1984 presidential election?

Q3 What college did Ronald Reagan attend?

Q4 'A Time for Choosing' was a speech by Ronald Reagan supporting what presidential candidate?

Q5 Who was appointed Chief Justice of the Supreme Court during Ronald Reagan's presidency?

Q6 Who was the leader of the Soviet Union during the second half of Ronald Reagan's presidency?

Q7 What 1938 film did Ronald Reagan co-star in with Jane Wyman?

Q8 What political party was Ronald Reagan a member of before 1962?

Q9 What US state did Ronald Reagan fail to win in the 1984 presidential election?

Q10 Ronald Reagan had a strong relationship with what British Prime Minister?

Ronald Reagan 3 (expert)

Q1 How many times did Ronald Reagan run unsuccessfully for the Republican nomination for President?

Q2 What disease was Ronald Reagan diagnosed with in the 1990s?

Q3 Ronald Reagan served as the 9th and 13th President of what?

Q4 In what year was the Intermediate-Range Nuclear Forces Treaty signed?

Q5 How many children did Ronald Reagan have?

Q6 What CBS anthology series did Ronald Reagan become the host of during the 1950s?

Q7 Where is the Ronald Reagan Presidential Library located?

Q8 In what year did Ronald Reagan die?

Q9 The Bitburg controversy occurred during a visit by Ronald Reagan to commemorate what?

Q10 What country did the USA invade in 1983?

George H W Bush 1 (easy)

Q1 What does the H W stand for in George H W Bush's name?

    A Harry Wilson
    B Herbert Walker
    C Henry William
    D Houdini Warren

Q2 What US state was George H W Bush born in?

    A Texas
    B Massachusetts
    C Vermont
    D Nevada

Q3 What was the name of George H W Bush's wife?

    A Samantha
    B Georgie
    C Jane
    D Barbara

Q4 What university did George H W Bush attend?

    A Harvard University
    B Yale University
    C Princeton University
    D Brown University

Q5 George H W Bush served as Vice President under what President?

    A Dwight Eisenhower
    B Jimmy Carter
    C Gerald Ford
    D Ronald Reagan

Q6 George H W Bush and his wife both died in what year?

  A 2005
  B 2009
  C 2012
  D 2018

Q7 Who served as Vice President during George H W Bush's presidency?

  A Dick Cheney
  B Nelson Rockefeller
  C Dan Quayle
  D Bill Clinton

Q8 Who did George H W Bush defeat in the 1988 presidential election?

  A Chuck Schumer
  B Michael Dukakis
  C Jimmy Carter
  D Mitt Romney

Q9 What wall fell during George H W Bush's presidency?

  A Antonine Wall
  B US-Mexico Border Wall
  C Berlin Wall
  D Hadrian's Wall

Q10 Which of the following wars broke out during George H W Bush's presidency?

  A Iraq War
  B Gulf War
  C Vietnam War
  D Soviet-Afghan War

George H W Bush 2 (average)

Q1 Which of George H W Bush's sons served as Governor of Florida?

Q2 George H W Bush served as the Ambassador to what between 1971 and 1973?

Q3 What intelligence service was George H W Bush the Director of?

Q4 Who defeated George H W Bush in the 1992 presidential election?

Q5 What political party was George H W Bush a member of during his presidency?

Q6 George H W Bush postponed his university studies after what historical event?

Q7 What relation is George W Bush to George H W Bush?

Q8 What war did George H W Bush serve in?

Q9 What was George H W Bush's maternal grandfather called?

Q10 What union was broken up during George H W Bush's presidency?

George H W Bush 3 (expert)

Q1 What agreement did the North American Free Trade Agreement supersede?

Q2 What was George H W Bush's military rank?

Q3 What ruler of Panama did George H W Bush's administration depose?

Q4 What did George H W Bush's eldest daughter, Pauline Robinson Bush, die from at the age of 3?

Q5 What secret society was George H W Bush a member of while at university?

Q6 How many judges did George H W Bush successfully appoint to the Supreme Court?

Q7 How many people served as Secretary of State in George H W Bush's administration?

Q8 What Congress covered the first two years of George H W Bush's presidency?

Q9 Operation Restore Hope concerned what country?

Q10 Who ran as an independent candidate in the 1992 presidential election?

Bill Clinton 1 (easy)

Q1 What is Bill Clinton's middle name?

    A Fred
    B David
    C Jefferson
    D Daniel

Q2 What is the name of Bill Clinton's wife?

    A Lucy
    B Fiona
    C Clara
    D Hillary

Q3 Who served as Vice President under Bill Clinton?

    A Al Gore
    B John Kerry
    C Frank White
    D Nancy Pelosi

Q4 Bill Clinton served as Governor of what US state?

    A Arkansas
    B Delaware
    C South Carolina
    D California

Q5 In what year was the impeachment of Bill Clinton initiated by the House of Representatives?

    A 1994
    B 1996
    C 1998
    D 2000

Q6 What is the name of Bill Clinton's daughter?

    A Chelsea
    B Dana
    C Gabrielle
    D Penelope

Q7 What English university did Bill Clinton attend?

    A Oxford University
    B University of Leicester
    C Durham University
    D Cambridge University

Q8 As a university student, Bill Clinton protested against what war?

    A Korean War
    B Vietnam War
    C Soviet-Afghan War
    D Gulf War

Q9 Who served as Bill Clinton's first Secretary of State?

    A John Kerry
    B Hillary Clinton
    C Warren Christopher
    D Rex Tillerson

Q10 Bill Clinton is often associated with what instrument?

    A Banjo
    B Guitar
    C Saxophone
    D Drums

Bill Clinton 2 (average)

Q1 What political party was Bill Clinton a member of during his presidency?

Q2 What two opponents did Bill Clinton face in the 1996 presidential election?

Q3 What White House intern did Bill Clinton have an affair with?

Q4 Bill Clinton met Hillary Clinton at what university?

Q5 Bill Clinton was the first President from what generation?

Q6 How many other Presidents had been impeached before Bill Clinton?

Q7 What non-profit organisation did Bill Clinton establish in 1997?

Q8 In what year of Bill Clinton's presidency did the Republicans gain majorities in both houses of houses of Congress?

Q9 What is the title of Bill Clinton's autobiography?

Q10 Which relative of Bill Clinton died three months before he was born?

Bill Clinton 3 (expert)

Q1 In what year was the Gramm–Leach–Bliley Act passed?

Q2 The 2000 Camp David Summit was a summit meeting involving what three individuals?

Q3 What city was Bill Clinton born in?

Q4 How many judges did Bill Clinton successfully appoint to the Supreme Court?

Q5 What was Bill Clinton's birth name?

Q6 What was Roger Clinton Sr.'s occupation?

Q7 How many people has Bill Clinton's mother been married to?

Q8 In what year did the White House travel office controversy (Travelgate) begin?

Q9 What law firm provided Bill Clinton's defence during the impeachment proceedings against him?

Q10 On 22nd September 1993, Bill Clinton made a major speech to Congress regarding what?

George W Bush 1 (easy)

Q1 George W Bush served as Governor of what US state?

A Nevada
B California
C Massachusetts
D Texas

Q2 What does the W stand for in George W Bush's name?

A Watson
B Walker
C Walter
D Wayne

Q3 What is the name of George W Bush's wife?

A Stacey
B Laura
C Riley
D Zara

Q4 What university did George W Bush graduate from in 1968?

A Brown University
B Wake Forest University
C Yale University
D University of Mississippi

Q5 Who won the popular vote in the 2000 presidential election?

A George W Bush
B Bill Clinton
C John Kerry
D Al Gore

Q6 What city was George W Bush born in?

    A Boston, Massachusetts
    B Houston, Texas
    C New Haven, Connecticut
    D Honolulu, Hawaii

Q7 George Bush co-owned what Major League Baseball team?

    A St Louis Cardinals
    B San Francisco Giants
    C Los Angeles Angels
    D Texas Rangers

Q8 What happened on 11th September 2001?

    A Invasion of Iraq
    B George W Bush's inauguration
    C Terrorist attack
    D George H W Bush's death

Q9 What war took place during George W Bush's presidency?

    A Soviet-Afghan War
    B Gulf War
    C Iraq War
    D Syrian Civil War

Q10 The Bush Doctrine refers to various principles of what kind of policy?

    A Religious policy
    B Foreign policy
    C Racial policy
    D Health policy

George W Bush 2 (average)

Q1 How many terms did George W Bush serve as President?

Q2 Who served as Vice President during George W Bush's presidency?

Q3 George W Bush's brother, Jeb Bush, served as Governor of what US state?

Q4 Who did George W Bush successfully appoint Chief Justice of the Supreme Court?

Q5 George W Bush's administration's response to what 2005 hurricane was heavily criticised?

Q6 What is the name of George W Bush's 2010 memoir?

Q7 The George W. Bush Presidential Center is located on the campus of what university?

Q8 What term did George W Bush use to describe foreign governments that sponsor terrorism and seek weapons of mass destruction?

Q9 What dictator was overthrown during the Iraq War?

Q10 What relation is George H W Bush to George W Bush?

George W Bush 3 (expert)

Q1 What was the code name of the War in Afghanistan?

Q2 What is the full name of the USA PATRIOT Act?

Q3 How many children does George W Bush have?

Q4 In what year did the investment bank Lehman Brothers collapse?

Q5 What Georgian national attempted to assassinate George W Bush?

Q6 What book did George W Bush release about his father in 2014?

Q7 Where were the 2002 Winter Olympics held?

Q8 What controversy involved six purported documents that were critical of George W Bush's service in the Texas Air National Guard?

Q9 George W Bush's family were members of what church?

Q10 What hobby did George W Bush take up after leaving the White House?

Barack Obama 1 (easy)

Q1 Barack Obama served as a Senator from what US state?

    A Hawaii
    B New York
    C Illinois
    D Alabama

Q2 Barack Obama was the first person from what background to serve as President?

    A Working class
    B African American
    C Mormon
    D Circus

Q3 What is the name of Barack Obama's wife?

    A Linda
    B Michelle
    C Reyna
    D Princess

Q4 Who served as Vice President during Barack Obama's presidency?

    A Hillary Clinton
    B John Kerry
    C Chuck Schumer
    D Joe Biden

Q5 What country was Barack Obama's father, Barack Obama Sr., from?

    A USA
    B United Kingdom
    C Kenya
    D Syria

Q6 What is Barack Obama's middle name?

    A Isaac
    B Thomas
    C Hussein
    D Ibn

Q7 Who was Barack Obama's opponent in the 2008 presidential election?

    A Mitch McConnell
    B John McCain
    C Mitt Romney
    D Lindsey Graham

Q8 What was Barack Obama's political affiliation during his presidency?

    A Democratic Party
    B Republican Party
    C Libertarian Party
    D Independent

Q9 What university did Barack Obama graduate from in 1983?

    A Columbia University
    B Princeton University
    C Stanford University
    D University of Notre Dame

Q10 What was the Patient Protection and Affordable Care Act nicknamed?

    A Obamacare
    B National Health Service
    C Social Security
    D Safety Net

Barack Obama 2 (average)

Q1 What city was Barack Obama born in?

Q2 How many terms did Barack Obama serve as President?

Q3 Who was Barack Obama's principal opponent in the 2008 Democratic presidential primaries?

Q4 New START is a treaty between the USA and what other country?

Q5 Barack Obama ordered military intervention in what country in 2011?

Q6 What terrorist was killed on 2nd May 2011?

Q7 *Obergefell v. Hodges* was a landmark Supreme Court case relating to what issue?

Q8 At what school did a shooting occur on 14th December 2012?

Q9 What major international climate agreement was signed in 2016?

Q10 Barack Obama had sanctions placed on Russia for its military intervention in what country?

Barack Obama 3 (expert)

Q1 In what year did Barack Obama receive the Nobel Peace Prize?

Q2 Barack Obama served as a teacher at what law school?

Q3 How many Justices did Barack Obama successfully appoint to the Supreme Court?

Q4 In 2016, Barack Obama became the first President to visit what country since 1928?

Q5 How many people served as Secretary of State during Barack Obama's presidency?

Q6 Who did Barack Obama defeat in 2004 to become a US Senator?

Q7 Where was the 2008 Democratic National Convention held?

Q8 What are the names of Barack Obama's two pet Portuguese Water Dogs?

Q9 What Major League Baseball team does Barack Obama support?

Q10 What form of Christianity does Barack Obama follow?

Donald Trump 1 (easy)

Q1 How many times has Donald Trump got married?

 A 0
 B 1
 C 2
 D 3

Q2 What is Donald Trump's middle name?

 A Jeremiah
 B Jordan
 C John
 D James

Q3 Who did Donald Trump defeat in the 2016 presidential election?

 A Barack Obama
 B Mitt Romney
 C Hillary Clinton
 D Bernie Sanders

Q4 What is Donald Trump's nickname for Ted Cruz?

 A The Canadian
 B Terrible Ted
 C Trustworthy Ted
 D Lyin' Ted

Q5 In what city did the 2016 Republican National Convention take place?

 A Indianapolis, Indiana
 B Cleveland, Ohio
 C New York City, New York
 D Denver, Colorado

Q6 Who was Donald Trump's running mate in the 2016 presidential election?

A Mike Pence
B Mary Fallin
C Sarah Palin
D Paul Ryan

Q7 What is the name of Donald Trump's First Lady?

A Melania
B Susan
C Mandy
D Brenda

Q8 What political position did Donald Trump hold before becoming President?

A Secretary of State
B Senator
C State Governor
D None

Q9 What US state was Donald Trump born in?

A Illinois
B Texas
C Maryland
D New York

Q10 What was significant about Donald Trump becoming President?

A Oldest person to become President
B First President without a background in law
C First bachelor President
D First independent President

Donald Trump 2 (average)

Q1 Who served as Donald Trump's first Secretary of State?

Q2 What position did Sean Spicer hold in Donald Trump's administration?

Q3 What 1987 book did Donald Trump co-author with Tony Schwartz?

Q4 Donald Trump starred on what reality TV show for over a decade?

Q5 What was the name of the FBI director who Donald Trump dismissed in 2017?

Q6 What was Donald Trump's 2016 campaign slogan?

Q7 What city did Donald Trump's administration controversially recognise as being the capital of Israel?

Q8 Where did Donald Trump meet Kim Jong Un for the first time?

Q9 Donald Trump said 'I love the poorly educated' while making a speech in what US state?

Q10 What Justice did Donald Trump successfully appoint to the Supreme Court in 2018?

Donald Trump 3 (expert)

Q1 What was Executive Order 13769?

Q2 What proposed trade agreement between Australia, Brunei, Canada, Chile, Japan, Malaysia, Mexico, New Zealand, Peru, Singapore, Vietnam, and the United States did Donald Trump's administration withdraw from?

Q3 What former lawyer of Donald Trump was sentenced to 3 years in prison in December 2018?

Q4 What business school did Donald Trump attend?

Q5 What palace did Donald Trump meet Queen Elizabeth II at in his first presidential visit to the United Kingdom?

Q6 Who served as Attorney General between 2017 and 2018?

Q7 Which Senator and former prisoner of war did Donald Trump attack in the early stages of his presidential campaign?

Q8 Which party won the House of Representatives and which party won the Senate in the 2018 midterm elections?

Q9 A central pledge Donald Trump made in his presidential campaign was to build what?

Q10 What key Obama-era act relating to healthcare did Donald Trump vow to repeal and replace?

Answers

George Washington 1 (easy)

Q1 Independent
Q2 John Adams
Q3 Martha Washington
Q4 Stepson
Q5 2
Q6 Anglican
Q7 0
Q8 Military encampment
Q9 Mr President
Q10 Political parties

George Washington 2 (average)

Q1 Mount Vernon
Q2 Colony of Virginia
Q3 Continental Arm
Q4 100%
Q5 Plot to assassinate George Washington
Q6 Federal Hall, New York City
Q7 France
Q8 Delaware
Q9 Financial crisis
Q10 Barbados

George Washington 3 (expert)

Q1 1796
Q2 Mary Ball Washington and Augustine Washington
Q3 Ferry Farm
Q4 1889
Q5 George Washington's skull
Q6 Robert Dinwiddie
Q7 First Continental Congress
Q8 1790
Q9 Manhattan Island
Q10 Newburgh Conspiracy

John Adams 1 (easy)

Q1 Smith
Q2 Thomas Jefferson
Q3 United Kingdom and the Netherlands
Q4 1
Q5 Massachusetts
Q6 Vice President
Q7 France
Q8 6
Q9 29
Q10 USS *Constitution*

John Adams 2 (average)

Q1 Federalist Party
Q2 Thomas Pinckney
Q3 The White House
Q4 Harvard University
Q5 John Adams Sr.
Q6 Boston Massacre
Q7 USS *Boston*
Q8 Democratic-Republican
Q9 Quasi War
Q10 Thomas Jefferson and James Madison

John Adams 3 (expert)

Q1 Constitution of Massachusetts
Q2 1798
Q3 *The New England Primer*
Q4 The Stamp Act of 1765
Q5 Thomas Jefferson, Benjamin Franklin, Roger Sherman and Robert Livingston
Q6 Oliver Ellsworth
Q7 Peacefield
Q8 John Fries
Q9 1800
Q10 90

Thomas Jefferson 1 (easy)

Q1 Louisiana Territory
Q2 Virginia
Q3 Daughter
Q4 Alexander Hamilton
Q5 Lawyer
Q6 Secretary of State
Q7 South Dakota
Q8 Violin
Q9 France
Q10 Alexander Hamilton

Thomas Jefferson 2 (average)

Q1 College of William and Mary
Q2 Martha Jefferson
Q3 University of Virginia
Q4 United States Declaration of Independence?
Q5 Italy
Q6 *National Gazette*
Q7 John Marshall
Q8 3
Q9 Supreme Court of the United States
Q10 West Point

Thomas Jefferson 3 (expert)

Q1 1801-09
Q2 The Act Prohibiting Importation of Slaves
Q3 *Notes on the State of Virginia*
Q4 Sally Hemings
Q5 14
Q6 The Jefferson disc
Q7 Storming of the Bastille
Q8 1801
Q9 The First Barbary War
Q10 The *Chesapeake–Leopard* affair

James Madison 1 (easy)

Q1 Secretary of State
Q2 George Clinton
Q3 War of 1812
Q4 Philadelphia
Q5 Virginia
Q6 Stepson
Q7 Anglican
Q8 The Constitution
Q9 2
Q10 James Monroe

James Madison 2 (average)

Q1 John Jay and Alexander Hamilton
Q2 The Constitutional Convention
Q3 Charles Cotesworth Pinckney
Q4 No one
Q5 Montpelier
Q6 Dolley Madison
Q7 College of New Jersey (now Princeton University)
Q8 *The Federalist Papers*
Q9 0
Q10 Democratic-Republican Party

James Madison 3 (expert)

Q1 1816
Q2 James Madison Sr. and Eleanor Rose Conway
Q3 The Alien and Sedition Acts
Q4 5 ft 4
Q5 War of 1812
Q6 DeWitt Clinton
Q7 Washington D.C.
Q8 1825
Q9 1836
Q10 5th and 15th

James Monroe 1 (easy)

Q1 The Americas
Q2 Virginia dynasty
Q3 Democratic-Republican
Q4 Daniel D. Tompkins
Q5 Daughter
Q6 Financial crisis
Q7 Slavery
Q8 Liberia
Q9 New York
Q10 Independence Day

James Monroe 2 (average)

Q1 Battle of Trenton
Q2 2
Q3 Rufus King
Q4 Elizabeth Monroe
Q5 First Party System
Q6 Florida
Q7 College of William and Mary
Q8 Charlottesville, Virginia
Q9 2
Q10 United Kingdom

James Monroe 3 (expert)

Q1 1823
Q2 Joseph Jones
Q3 Kortright
Q4 United Kingdom and France
Q5 Argentina, Peru, Colombia, Chile and Mexico
Q6 Federalist Party
Q7 5
Q8 Massachusetts
Q9 Virginia Constitutional Convention of 1829–1830
Q10 1824

John Quincy Adams 1 (easy)

Q1 Father
Q2 Massachusetts
Q3 2
Q4 4
Q5 Andrew Jackson
Q6 4
Q7 Louisa Adams
Q8 4
Q9 London
Q10 Law book

John Quincy Adams 2 (average)

Q1 1
Q2 Congressman from Massachusetts
Q3 His great grandfather, John Quincy
Q4 Harvard University
Q5 An Associate Justice of the United States Supreme Court
Q6 Secretary of State
Q7 Henry Clay
Q8 John Adams
Q9 Eloquent
Q10 Father

John Quincy Adams 3 (expert)

Q1 The popular vote
Q2 All Hallows-by-the-Tower
Q3 Samuel Chase
Q4 Secretary of the Navy
Q5 1826
Q6 Monroe Doctrine
Q7 Ambassador to Prussia
Q8 Treaty of Ghent
Q9 United States v. The Amistad
Q10 Smithsonian Institution

Andrew Jackson 1 (easy)

Q1 Tennessee
Q2 2
Q3 1824
Q4 Democratic
Q5 South Carolina
Q6 Tears
Q7 Northern Ireland
Q8 Lawyer
Q9 Hickory
Q10 New Orleans

Andrew Jackson 2 (average)

Q1 Rachel Jackson
Q2 John C. Calhoun and Martin Van Buren
Q3 2
Q4 Nashville
Q5 Battle of New Orleans
Q6 The Second Bank of the United States
Q7 Mississippi River
Q8 Republic of Texas
Q9 United Kingdom and Spain
Q10 Financial crisis (The Panic of 1837)

Andrew Jackson 3 (expert)

Q1 Creek War
Q2 The Tariff of Abominations
Q3 1830
Q4 Lewis Robards
Q5 Tennessee and Kentucky
Q6 3
Q7 Presbyterianism
Q8 The Coffin Handbills
Q9 Richard Lawrence
Q10 John Marshall

Martin Van Buren 1 (easy)

Q1 1
Q2 Democratic
Q3 New York
Q4 Hannah Van Buren
Q5 Vice President
Q6 The Netherlands
Q7 Magician
Q8 Texas
Q9 5
Q10 2

Martin Van Buren 2 (average)

Q1 Daughter-in-law
Q2 Free Soil Party
Q3 Richard Mentor Johnson
Q4 United Kingdom
Q5 Union
Q6 John Forsyth
Q7 Whig
Q8 Second Seminole War
Q9 Spain
Q10 English

Martin Van Buren 3 (expert)

Q1 Abraham Van Buren
Q2 The Albany Regency
Q3 The Kinderhook Reformed Dutch Church (Kinderhook, New York)
Q4 4
Q5 Charles Ogle
Q6 Lilburn Boggs
Q7 The Blue Room
Q8 No one
Q9 Andrew Jackson
Q10 Era of Good Feelings

<u>William Henry Harrison 1 (easy)</u>

Q1 1 month
Q2 Whig
Q3 Indiana Territory
Q4 Anna Harrison
Q5 Pneumonia
Q6 University of Pennsylvania
Q7 Virginia
Q8 Tippecanoe
Q9 27th
Q10 Gran Colombia

<u>William Henry Harrison 2 (average)</u>

Q1 Berkeley Plantation
Q2 Benjamin Harrison
Q3 John Tyler
Q4 Cold weather at his inauguration
Q5 Roger B. Taney
Q6 Medical school
Q7 War of 1812
Q8 American Revolutionary War
Q9 Indiana
Q10 Daniel Webster

<u>William Henry Harrison 3 (expert)</u>

Q1 Campaign song (1840 presidential election)
Q2 Benjamin Harrison V
Q3 Wesley Chapel (Cincinnati, Ohio)
Q4 3
Q5 William Henry Harrison Tomb State Memorial
Q6 Symmes
Q7 Anthony Wayne
Q8 Vincennes University (founded as Jefferson Academy)
Q9 1809
Q10 Army of the Northwest

John Tyler 1 (easy)

Q1 1
Q2 Vice President
Q3 Virginia
Q4 3
Q5 Daughter-in-law
Q6 His Accidency
Q7 Whig
Q8 Law
Q9 Captain
Q10 Daniel Webster

John Tyler 2 (average)

Q1 Confederate States of America
Q2 The White House
Q3 Greenway Plantation
Q4 College of William and Mary
Q5 USS *Princeton*
Q6 Sherwood Forest
Q7 No one
Q8 Whig Party
Q9 British North American colonies (present-day Canada)
Q10 Republic of Texas

John Tyler 3 (expert)

Q1 Hollywood Cemetery
Q2 Letitia Christian Tyler and Julia Gardiner Tyler
Q3 American Civil War
Q4 7
Q5 Sioux City, Iowa
Q6 Samuel Nelson
Q7 'Doctor, I am going. Perhaps it is best.'
Q8 James Monroe (he is also buried near the President of the Confederate States of America, Jefferson Davis)

Q9 Henry Clay
Q10 27th and 28th Congress

James Polk 1 (easy)

Q1 Democratic
Q2 Samuel Polk
Q3 Tennessee
Q4 1
Q5 Hickory
Q6 Less than a year
Q7 George M. Dallas
Q8 Mexican-American War
Q9 Oregon
Q10 1848

James Polk 2 (average)

Q1 1
Q2 Sarah Childress Polk
Q3 North Carolina
Q4 Knox
Q5 Andrew Jackson
Q6 Henry Clay
Q7 Oregon Territory
Q8 University of North Carolina at Chapel Hill
Q9 0
Q10 James Buchanan

James Polk 3 (expert)

Q1 1846
Q2 Tennessee State Capitol
Q3 9
Q4 Cholera
Q5 Black Tariff
Q6 29th Congress
Q7 1835
Q8 Pledged to serve only 1 term in 1844 presidential election

Q9 2
Q10 Nashville

Zachary Taylor 1 (easy)

Q1 16 months
Q2 Margaret Taylor
Q3 Virginia
Q4 Whig
Q5 Old Whitey
Q6 Slavery
Q7 Soldier
Q8 United Kingdom
Q9 Mexican-American War
Q10 0

Zachary Taylor 2 (average)

Q1 Old Rough and Ready
Q2 Millard Fillmore
Q3 None
Q4 Lewis Cass
Q5 Richard Lee Taylor
Q6 Louisville
Q7 Martin Van Buren
Q8 Secretary of State
Q9 Utah
Q10 Mexico

Zachary Taylor 3 (expert)

Q1 William Brewster
Q2 Major General
Q3 1850
Q4 6
Q5 George W. Crawford
Q6 1875
Q7 Governor of Kentucky
Q8 *Tennessee*

Q9 Second Party System
Q10 Slavery

Millard Fillmore 1 (easy)

Q1 Whig
Q2 Vice President
Q3 New York
Q4 2
Q5 Abigail Fillmore
Q6 Lawyer
Q7 California
Q8 2
Q9 James Buchanan
Q10 Oxford University

Millard Fillmore 2 (average)

Q1 No one
Q2 0
Q3 Benjamin Robbins Curtis
Q4 Comptroller of New York
Q5 Matthew Calbraith Perry
Q6 Pope Pius IX
Q7 Secretary of State
Q8 William Cranch
Q9 Winfield Scott
Q10 1850

Millard Fillmore 3 (expert)

Q1 Forest Lawn Cemetery (Buffalo, New York)
Q2 Know Nothing
Q3 1800
Q4 1850-53
Q5 4
Q6 Cuba
Q7 The State University of New York at Buffalo
Q8 East Aurora

194

Q9 Brigham Young
Q10 George Brinton McClellan

Franklin Pierce 1 (easy)

Q1 Democratic
Q2 3
Q3 Jane Pierce
Q4 1854
Q5 New Hampshire
Q6 Vice President
Q7 Brother
Q8 Winfield Scott
Q9 Nathaniel Hawthorne
Q10 Jefferson Davis

Franklin Pierce 2 (average)

Q1 1
Q2 No one
Q3 Lawyer
Q4 New Hampshire
Q5 Secretary of State
Q6 New Mexico and Arizona
Q7 Stephen Douglas
Q8 Nicaragua
Q9 James Buchanan
Q10 Bleeding Kansas

Franklin Pierce 3 (expert)

Q1 Battle of Contreras
Q2 Bowdoin College
Q3 49th
Q4 Cuba
Q5 Old North Cemetery (Concord, New Hampshire)
Q6 Cirrhosis
Q7 Train accident
Q8 Austrian Empire

Q9 The Knights of the Golden Circle
Q10 Cuba

James Buchanan 1 (easy)

Q1 Buck
Q2 Democratic
Q3 Niece
Q4 American Civil War
Q5 Pennsylvania
Q6 Ambassador to the United Kingdom
Q7 4
Q8 Financial crisis
Q9 Baltimore
Q10 Edwin Stanton

James Buchanan 2 (average)

Q1 1
Q2 John Cabell Breckinridge
Q3 0
Q4 Dickinson College
Q5 Federalist
Q6 James Polk
Q7 Nathan Clifford
Q8 Utah Territory
Q9 3
Q10 Roger Brooke Taney

James Buchanan 3 (expert)

Q1 1857
Q2 John C Fremont and Millard Fillmore
Q3 Republican Party, Northern Democratic Party, Southern Democratic Party, and the Constitutional Union Party
Q4 Woodward Hill Cemetery (Lancaster, Pennsylvania)
Q5 Anne Caroline Coleman
Q6 Lancaster, Pennsylvania
Q7 Cincinnati

Q8 Andrew Jackson
Q9 Private
Q10 Charleston, South Carolina

Abraham Lincoln 1 (easy)

Q1 Charles Wilkes Booth
Q2 Republican
Q3 Kentucky
Q4 2
Q5 Antietam
Q6 1858
Q7 Jefferson Davis
Q8 11
Q9 Virginia
Q10 Lawyer

Abraham Lincoln 2 (average)

Q1 Illinois
Q2 Ford's Theatre
Q3 Mary Todd Lincoln
Q4 Hannibal Hamlin
Q5 2
Q6 Salmon Portland Chase
Q7 Secretary of State
Q8 Black Hawk War
Q9 Assassinate Abraham Lincoln
Q10 Winfield Scott

Abraham Lincoln 3 (expert)

Q1 William Wallace Lincoln
Q2 Oak Ridge Cemetery (Springfield, Illinois)
Q3 The *Trent* Affair
Q4 Ann Rutledge
Q5 1863
Q6 Galusha Aaron Grow
Q7 Reconstruction era

Q8 1862
Q9 First Transcontinental Railroad
Q10 New York City

Andrew Johnson 1 (easy)

Q1 National Union Party
Q2 0
Q3 Tennessee
Q4 Raleigh
Q5 Under 2 months
Q6 1868
Q7 Tailor
Q8 14th Amendment
Q9 President
Q10 Saving two men from drowning

Andrew Johnson 2 (average)

Q1 Eliza McCardle Johnson
Q2 Democratic
Q3 Lorenzo Thomas
Q4 Salmon Portland Chase
Q5 Hannibal Hamlin
Q6 George Atzerodt
Q7 Senator
Q8 Stroke
Q9 Colorado
Q10 Reconstruction era

Andrew Johnson 3 (expert)

Q1 1865-66
Q2 126
Q3 Edmund Gibson Ross
Q4 15th April 1865
Q5 William Seward
Q6 Greeneville, Tennessee
Q7 5

Q8 None
Q9 War Democrats
Q10 Brigadier General

Ulysses Grant 1 (easy)

Q1 Hiram
Q2 Ohio
Q3 Julia Grant
Q4 Yellowstone
Q5 15th
Q6 Embark on a world tour
Q7 St Louis, Missouri
Q8 1864
Q9 Horatio Seymour
Q10 Hamilton Fish

Ulysses Grant 2 (average)

Q1 2
Q2 West Point
Q3 Republican
Q4 Appomattox Court House
Q5 1862
Q6 Elihu Benjamin Washburne
Q7 William Howard Taft
Q8 Union Pacific Railroad
Q9 Chicago
Q10 Colorado

Ulysses Grant 3 (expert)

Q1 Schuyler Colfax and Henry Wilson
Q2 1872
Q3 *Mary and John*
Q4 Liberal Republican Party
Q5 Texas, Mississippi and Virginia
Q6 4
Q7 Ferdinand Ward

Q8 Mark Twain
Q9 1870
Q10 United Kingdom

Rutherford Hayes 1 (easy)

Q1 Birchard
Q2 Lucy
Q3 Ohio
Q4 Samuel Tilden
Q5 Battle of South Mountain
Q6 Pull remaining federal troops out of the South
Q7 Gilded Age
Q8 Railroad
Q9 Not yet born
Q10 John Hunt Morgan

Rutherford Hayes 2 (average)

Q1 1
Q2 Republican
Q3 Governor of Ohio
Q4 Bland–Allison Act
Q5 William Almon Wheeler
Q6 Harvard Law School
Q7 The Philippines
Q8 Major General
Q9 William McKinley
Q10 Oregon

Rutherford Hayes 3 (expert)

Q1 Lemonade Lucy
Q2 Spiegel Grove
Q3 8
Q4 23rd
Q5 70
Q6 George Crook
Q7 The Red Room (in the White House)

Q8 William Evarts
Q9 Paraguay
Q10 The Coinage Act

James Garfield 1 (easy)

Q1 Chester Arthur
Q2 Secretary of State
Q3 Abram
Q4 Under a year
Q5 Lucretia
Q6 Preacher President
Q7 American Civil War
Q8 Congressman
Q9 Alexander Graham Bell
Q10 In a log cabin

James Garfield 2 (average)

Q1 Assassination
Q2 Ohio
Q3 His mother
Q4 Theodore Roosevelt
Q5 The Christian Church (Disciples of Christ)
Q6 Williams College
Q7 Chicago, Illinois
Q8 Winfield Scott Hancock
Q9 Stanley Matthews
Q10 New Jersey

James Garfield 3 (expert)

Q1 Killing James Garfield
Q2 Lake View Cemetery (Cleveland, Ohio)
Q3 Baltimore and Potomac Railroad Station
Q4 1862
Q5 19th
Q6 Roscoe Conkling
Q7 Middle Creek, Shiloh and Chickamauga

Q8 36th
Q9 Collector of the Port of New York
Q10 Canal boat

Chester Arthur 1 (easy)

Q1 Alan
Q2 Vice President
Q3 Republican
Q4 Vermont
Q5 Sister
Q6 New York
Q7 Northern Ireland
Q8 Kidneys
Q9 3
Q10 Frederick Theodore Frelinghuysen

Chester Arthur 2 (average)

Q1 Ellen 'Nell' Arthur
Q2 No one
Q3 James Gillespie Blaine
Q4 Union College
Q5 New York
Q6 George Hunt Pendleton
Q7 Brigadier general
Q8 1
Q9 Civil Rights Act of 1875
Q10 William Eaton Chandler

Chester Arthur 3 (expert)

Q1 John Riker Brady
Q2 1883
Q3 Albany Rural Cemetery
Q4 1882
Q5 Erastus Dean Culver
Q6 Collector of the Port of New York
Q7 2

Q8 Roscoe Conkling
Q9 France
Q10 0

Grover Cleveland 1 (easy)

Q1 Serve non-consecutive terms
Q2 Democratic
Q3 New Jersey
Q4 Rose Cleveland
Q5 2
Q6 James Gillespie Blaine
Q7 Buffalo
Q8 3
Q9 Presbyterian minister
Q10 United Kingdom

Grover Cleveland 2 (average)

Q1 Indianapolis
Q2 Governor of New York
Q3 Railroad
Q4 Lawyer
Q5 Gray Gables
Q6 Washington D.C.
Q7 Hawaii
Q8 Venezuela
Q9 Cancer
Q10 Utah

Grover Cleveland 3 (expert)

Q1 1886
Q2 1893
Q3 Baby Ruth
Q4 Mugwumps
Q5 Third Party System
Q6 4
Q7 The McKinley Tariff

Q8 Washington, Montana, North Dakota and South Dakota
Q9 Heart attack
Q10 3

Benjamin Harrison 1 (easy)

Q1 Indiana
Q2 Great Grandfather
Q3 Republican
Q4 Grover Cleveland
Q5 2
Q6 Ohio
Q7 Daughter
Q8 6
Q9 Influenza
Q10 Miami University

Benjamin Harrison 2 (average)

Q1 1
Q2 Levi Parsons Morton
Q3 William Henry Harrison
Q4 Lawyer
Q5 William Howard Taft
Q6 Indianapolis, Indiana
Q7 Congressman
Q8 James Garfield
Q9 Chicago
Q10 Venezuela

Benjamin Harrison 3 (expert)

Q1 1892
Q2 McKinley Tariff
Q3 1890
Q4 70th Indiana Infantry Regiment
Q5 Cincinnati
Q6 4
Q7 His wife, Caroline Harrison

Q8 Populist Party
Q9 Chile
Q10 The Shoshone National Forest

William McKinley 1 (easy)

Q1 Buffalo
Q2 Garret Hobart
Q3 Ohio
Q4 Electric chair
Q5 Ida
Q6 American Civil War
Q7 William Jennings Bryan
Q8 Spanish-American War
Q9 Major
Q10 Methodist

William McKinley 2 (average)

Q1 Leon Czolgosz
Q2 2
Q3 Governor of Ohio
Q4 Melville Weston Fuller
Q5 0
Q6 Lawyer
Q7 William Jennings Bryan
Q8 Congressman
Q9 Secretary of State
Q10 USS *Maine*

William McKinley 3 (expert)

Q1 Pan-American Exposition
Q2 1898
Q3 Paris, France
Q4 Mark Hanna
Q5 1900
Q6 23rd Regiment, Ohio Volunteer Infantry
Q7 1873

Q8 3
Q9 Gold Democrats (National Democratic Party)
Q10 China

Theodore Roosevelt 1 (easy)

Q1 New York City
Q2 Vice President
Q3 Progressive Era
Q4 Republican
Q5 2
Q6 New York
Q7 Brazil
Q8 5
Q9 Rough Riders
Q10 Spanish-American War

Theodore Roosevelt 2 (average)

Q1 John Raymond Hazel
Q2 Alton Brooks Parker
Q3 Progressive Party
Q4 Edith Roosevelt
Q5 Charles Warren Fairbanks
Q6 Medal of Honor
Q7 Panama Canal
Q8 Big stick
Q9 Roosevelt Corollary
Q10 Republic of Panama

Theodore Roosevelt 3 (expert)

Q1 The Ansley Wilcox House
Q2 Bright's disease
Q3 *The Naval War of 1812*
Q4 Sagamore Hill
Q5 Mayor of New York City
Q6 Martha Bulloch Roosevelt (his mother) and Alice Hathaway Roosevelt (his wife)
Q7 *The Harvard Advocate*

Q8 William Howard Taft
Q9 Russo-Japanese War
Q10 Square Deal

William Howard Taft 1 (easy)

Q1 James Sherman
Q2 Cincinnati
Q3 Helen
Q4 Socialist
Q5 Chief Justice of the Supreme Court
Q6 Secretary of War
Q7 Yale University
Q8 William McKinley
Q9 Lawyer
Q10 5

William Howard Taft 2 (average)

Q1 1
Q2 Republican
Q3 Philander Chase Knox
Q4 William Jennings Bryan
Q5 Alphonso Taft
Q6 Ohio
Q7 Temperance movement
Q8 Melville Fuller
Q9 Secretary of Agriculture
Q10 Banana Wars

William Howard Taft 3 (expert)

Q1 William Howard Taft, Woodrow Wilson, Theodore Roosevelt and Eugene Debs
Q2 Arizona and New Mexico
Q3 Arlington National Cemetery
Q4 Skull and Bones
Q5 U.S. Secretary of the Interior, Richard Achilles Ballinger
Q6 Edward Douglass White
Q7 1913

Q8 Payne–Aldrich Tariff Act
Q9 Dollar diplomacy
Q10 3

Woodrow Wilson 1 (easy)

Q1 First World War
Q2 Princeton University
Q3 Thomas Riley Marshall
Q4 Virginia
Q5 League of Nations
Q6 18th
Q7 New Jersey
Q8 3
Q9 Daughter
Q10 Kidneys

Woodrow Wilson 2 (average)

Q1 Democratic
Q2 2
Q3 Charles Evans Hughes
Q4 Wilsonianism
Q5 Fourteen Points
Q6 Progressive Era
Q7 Germany and Mexico
Q8 John Hopkins University
Q9 1912
Q10 Confederate States of America

Woodrow Wilson 3 (expert)

Q1 1913
Q2 1913
Q3 Stroke
Q4 Went on a tour of the USA
Q5 Phi Kappa Psi
Q6 Colorado Coalfield War
Q7 Jones–Shafroth Act

Q8 Selective Service Act of 1917
Q9 Woodrow Wilson (USA), David Lloyd George (United Kingdom), Vittorio Emanuele Orlando (Italy), and Georges Clemenceau (France)
Q10 Henry Cabot Lodge

Warren Harding 1 (easy)

Q1 Gamaliel
Q2 San Francisco
Q3 Florence
Q4 Republican
Q5 Senator
Q6 James Middleton Cox
Q7 A political scandal
Q8 Normalcy
Q9 Mistress
Q10 Secretary of State

Warren Harding 2 (average)

Q1 Ohio
Q2 Calvin Coolidge
Q3 Chicago, Illinois
Q4 1921-23
Q5 Daughter
Q6 1
Q7 Secretary of Commerce
Q8 Edward Douglass White
Q9 William Howard Taft
Q10 Heart attack

Warren Harding 3 (expert)

Q1 *The Marion Star*
Q2 10th
Q3 4
Q4 5
Q5 Ohio Central College
Q6 Black

Q7 World War One
Q8 1921
Q9 1922
Q10 Great Railroad Strike of 1922

Calvin Coolidge 1 (easy)

Q1 Business
Q2 Vice President
Q3 Massachusetts
Q4 Tennis
Q5 Grace
Q6 Roaring Twenties
Q7 Coolidge Homestead
Q8 1
Q9 Father
Q10 15

Calvin Coolidge 2 (average)

Q1 Vermont
Q2 Republican
Q3 Charles Gates Dawes
Q4 Boston Police Strike
Q5 Coolidge Homestead
Q6 Amherst College
Q7 Massachusetts
Q8 Silent Cal
Q9 Independence Day
Q10 Mississippi River

Calvin Coolidge 3 (expert)

Q1 John William Davis and Robert Marion La Follette
Q2 Phi Gamma Delta
Q3 Plymouth Notch Cemetery
Q4 John Coolidge
Q5 McNary–Haugen Farm Relief Bill
Q6 2

Q7 1924
Q8 'I do not choose to run'
Q9 1929
Q10 Alcohol

Herbert Hoover 1 (easy)

Q1 Al Smith
Q2 Charles Curtis
Q3 Iowa
Q4 Secretary of Commerce
Q5 Lou
Q6 Belgium
Q7 Quaker
Q8 Stanford University
Q9 Uncle
Q10 Mining

Herbert Hoover 2 (average)

Q1 Republican
Q2 1932
Q3 Wall Street Crash of 1929
Q4 William Howard Taft
Q5 The Boxer Rebellion
Q6 Smoot–Hawley Tariff Act
Q7 Gold standard
Q8 Secretary of State
Q9 The Bonus Army
Q10 Adolf Hitler

Herbert Hoover 3 (expert)

Q1 1936
Q2 Kansas City
Q3 1964
Q4 Geology
Q5 2
Q6 1929

Q7 Hooverville
Q8 Severino Di Giovanni
Q9 1931
Q10 Fourth Party System

Franklin Roosevelt 1 (easy)

Q1 Delano
Q2 4
Q3 Great Depression
Q4 New Deal
Q5 Eleanor
Q6 New York
Q7 State Governor
Q8 James Cox
Q9 1945
Q10 Paralytic

Franklin Roosevelt 2 (average)

Q1 Democratic
Q2 3
Q3 Springwood Estate
Q4 Navy
Q5 Japanese attack on Pearl Harbor
Q6 Series of evening radio addresses by Franklin Roosevelt
Q7 Fear itself
Q8 Shangri-La
Q9 Germany, Italy and Japan
Q10 1941

Franklin Roosevelt 3 (expert)

Q1 Fifth cousins
Q2 Frances Perkins
Q3 Lucy Mercer
Q4 The Little White House (Warm Springs, Georgia)
Q5 Twenty-first Amendment to the United States Constitution
Q6 Alf Landon

Q7 Add more Supreme Court Justices
Q8 1935
Q9 Harry Hopkins
Q10 The Works Progress Administration

Harry Truman 1 (easy)

Q1 Missouri
Q2 Elizabeth
Q3 1945
Q4 United Kingdom
Q5 Senator
Q6 Second World War
Q7 Korean War
Q8 1
Q9 Cold War
Q10 New Mexico

Harry Truman 2 (average)

Q1 Democratic
Q2 Alben William Barkley
Q3 Marshall Plan
Q4 Hiroshima and Nagasaki
Q5 Soviet Union
Q6 Kansas City
Q7 First World War
Q8 Margaret Truman
Q9 George Catlett Marshall Jr.
Q10 Nuremberg trials

Harry Truman 3 (expert)

Q1 Thomas Dewey and Storm Thurmond
Q2 1948-49
Q3 Executive Order 9981
Q4 University of Missouri–Kansas City School of Law
Q5 Trinity
Q6 1945-46

Q7 White House Press Secretary
Q8 Philadelphia, Pennsylvania
Q9 Douglas MacArthur
Q10 Blair House

Dwight Eisenhower 1 (easy)

Q1 Africa
Q2 Republican
Q3 Richard Nixon
Q4 Mamie
Q5 Ambassador to Belgium
Q6 Texas
Q7 Ike
Q8 General of the Army
Q9 David
Q10 American Football

Dwight Eisenhower 2 (average)

Q1 Adlai Ewing Stevenson II
Q2 Frederick Moore Vinson
Q3 West Point
Q4 Middle East
Q5 Korean War
Q6 Grandson
Q7 Columbia University
Q8 John Foster Dulles
Q9 Earl Warren
Q10 New Look

Dwight Eisenhower 3 (expert)

Q1 1953-61
Q2 2
Q3 The George Washington Inaugural Bible and Dwight Eisenhower's personal Bible
Q4 The class the stars fell on
Q5 1954
Q6 1951-52

Q7 Augusta National Golf Club
Q8 The Bay of Pigs Invasion
Q9 Joseph McCarthy
Q10 Federal Aid Highway Act of 1956

John Kennedy 1 (easy)

Q1 Fitzgerald
Q2 Robert
Q3 Dallas
Q4 Massachusetts
Q5 Jacqueline
Q6 Vice President
Q7 Second World War
Q8 October
Q9 Nomination speech
Q10 50

John Kennedy 2 (average)

Q1 Democratic
Q2 Lee Harvey Oswald
Q3 Harvard University
Q4 Richard Nixon
Q5 Secretary of State
Q6 Brookline, Massachusetts
Q7 Roman Catholic
Q8 Theodore Roosevelt
Q9 Cuba
Q10 Yuri Gagarin

John Kennedy 3 (expert)

Q1 22nd November 1963
Q2 1961
Q3 Parkland Memorial Hospital
Q4 Joseph Patrick Kennedy and Rose Kennedy
Q5 *Profiles in Courage*
Q6 Warren Commission

Q7 Eternal flame
Q8 Plane crash
Q9 Inga Arvad
Q10 They were televised

Lyndon Johnson 1 (easy)

Q1 Texas
Q2 Democratic
Q3 Baines
Q4 Great Society
Q5 Claudia
Q6 Vietnam War
Q7 Hubert Humphrey
Q8 Senate Majority Leader
Q9 War on Poverty
Q10 Navy

Lyndon Johnson 2 (average)

Q1 Barry Goldwater
Q2 Stonewall, Texas
Q3 Lady Bird
Q4 1
Q5 Secretary of Defence
Q6 USS *Maddox*
Q7 Samuel Ealy Johnson Jr.
Q8 Texas State University
Q9 Dean Rusk
Q10 Richard Nixon

Lyndon Johnson 3 (expert)

Q1 1964
Q2 4th
Q3 1964
Q4 Hubert Humphrey
Q5 Montgomery, Alabama
Q6 Corporation for Public Broadcasting

Q7 1974
Q8 Atlantic City, New Jersey
Q9 University of Texas at Austin
Q10 Long, hot summer of 1967

Richard Nixon 1 (easy)

Q1 Milhous
Q2 2
Q3 Dwight Eisenhower
Q4 Patricia
Q5 California
Q6 Second World War
Q7 Soviet Union
Q8 Israel
Q9 1974
Q10 Apollo 11

Richard Nixon 2 (average)

Q1 Republican
Q2 Hubert Humphrey and George Wallace
Q3 Governor of California
Q4 Environmental Protection Agency
Q5 Spiro Agnew
Q6 Chile
Q7 George McGovern
Q8 Watergate scandal
Q9 Warren Earl Burger
Q10 Richard the Lionheart

Richard Nixon 3 (expert)

Q1 La Casa Pacifica
Q2 Alger Hiss
Q3 1972
Q4 Cancer
Q5 Yorba Linda, California
Q6 Gerald Ford

Q7 A stroke
Q8 Duke University
Q9 Commander
Q10 William Pierce Rogers

Gerald Ford 1 (easy)

Q1 0
Q2 Nelson Rockefeller
Q3 Rudolph
Q4 25th
Q5 Nebraska
Q6 Navy
Q7 Elizabeth
Q8 Gerald
Q9 Vietnam War
Q10 895

Gerald Ford 2 (average)

Q1 Republican
Q2 Jimmy Carter
Q3 Father
Q4 Eagle Scout
Q5 American Football
Q6 University of Michigan
Q7 Warren Commission
Q8 House Minority Leader
Q9 Spiro Agnew
Q10 Korean

Gerald Ford 3 (expert)

Q1 3202 Woolworth Avenue, Omaha, Nebraska
Q2 Grand Rapids, Michigan
Q3 Leslie Lynch King Jr.
Q4 Lieutenant Commander
Q5 1975
Q6 Delta Kappa Epsilon

218

Q7 Golden Retriever
Q8 Swine flu
Q9 2
Q10 John Paul Stevens

Jimmy Carter 1 (easy)

Q1 Georgia
Q2 Earl
Q3 Rosalynn
Q4 State Governor
Q5 Walter Mondale
Q6 Navy
Q7 0
Q8 Vietnam War
Q9 Iran
Q10 Pennsylvania

Jimmy Carter 2 (average)

Q1 Gerald Ford
Q2 Democratic
Q3 Nobel Peace Prize
Q4 Egypt and Israel
Q5 Afghanistan
Q6 1980 Summer Olympics, Moscow
Q7 Secretary of State
Q8 Panama Canal
Q9 2
Q10 Iran hostage crisis

Jimmy Carter 3 (expert)

Q1 Department of Energy and Department of Education
Q2 1982
Q3 United States Naval Academy
Q4 1979
Q5 Persian Gulf
Q6 Edward Moore Kennedy

Q7 *What's My Line?*
Q8 1978
Q9 Sub-Saharan Africa
Q10 Cancer

Ronald Reagan 1 (easy)

Q1 Illinois
Q2 Republican
Q3 Nancy Reagan
Q4 California
Q5 George Herbert Walker Bush
Q6 Actor
Q7 Reaganomics
Q8 John Hinckley Jr.
Q9 West Berlin
Q10 Air Force

Ronald Reagan 2 (average)

Q1 Jane Wyman
Q2 Walter Mondale
Q3 Eureka College
Q4 Barry Goldwater
Q5 William Rehnquist
Q6 Mikhail Gorbachev
Q7 *Brother Rat*
Q8 Democratic
Q9 Minnesota
Q10 Margaret Thatcher

Ronald Reagan 3 (expert)

Q1 2
Q2 Alzheimer's
Q3 Screen Actors Guild
Q4 1987
Q5 5
Q6 *General Electric Theatre*

Q7 Simi Valley, California
Q8 2004
Q9 The end of the Second World War
Q10 Grenada

George H W Bush 1 (easy)

Q1 Herbert Walker
Q2 Massachusetts
Q3 Barbara
Q4 Yale University
Q5 Ronald Reagan
Q6 2018
Q7 Dan Quayle
Q8 Michael Dukakis
Q9 Berlin Wall
Q10 Gulf War

George H W Bush 2 (average)

Q1 John Ellis 'Jeb' Bush
Q2 United Nations
Q3 Central Intelligence Agency (CIA)
Q4 Bill Clinton
Q5 Republican
Q6 Japanese attack on Pearl Harbor
Q7 Son
Q8 Second World War
Q9 George Herbert Walker
Q10 Soviet Union

George H W Bush 3 (expert)

Q1 Canada–United States Free Trade Agreement
Q2 Lieutenant
Q3 Manuel Noriega
Q4 Leukaemia
Q5 Skull and Bones
Q6 2

Q7 2
Q8 101ˢᵗ United States Congress
Q9 Somalia
Q10 Ross Perot

Bill Clinton 1 (easy)

Q1 Jefferson
Q2 Hillary
Q3 Al Gore
Q4 Arkansas
Q5 1998
Q6 Chelsea
Q7 Oxford University
Q8 Vietnam War
Q9 Warren Christopher
Q10 Saxophone

Bill Clinton 2 (average)

Q1 Democratic
Q2 Bob Dole and Ross Perot
Q3 Monica Lewinsky
Q4 Yale University
Q5 Baby boomer
Q6 1
Q7 Clinton Foundation
Q8 1994
Q9 *My Life*
Q10 Father

Bill Clinton 3 (expert)

Q1 1999
Q2 Bill Clinton (President of USA), Ehud Barak (Prime Minister of Israel) and Yasser Arafat (Palestinian Authority chairman)
Q3 Hope, Arkansas
Q4 2
Q5 William Jefferson Blythe III

Q6 Car salesman
Q7 4
Q8 1993
Q9 Williams & Connolly
Q10 Healthcare reform plan

George W Bush 1 (easy)

Q1 Texas
Q2 Walker
Q3 Laura
Q4 Yale University
Q5 Al Gore
Q6 New Haven, Connecticut
Q7 Texas Rangers
Q8 Terrorist attack
Q9 Iraq War
Q10 Foreign policy

George W Bush 2 (average)

Q1 2
Q2 Dick Cheney
Q3 Florida
Q4 John Roberts
Q5 Hurricane Katrina
Q6 *Decision Points*
Q7 Southern Methodist University
Q8 Axis of evil
Q9 Saddam Hussein
Q10 Father

George W Bush 3 (expert)

Q1 Operation Enduring Freedom – Afghanistan
Q2 Uniting and Strengthening America by Providing Appropriate Tools Required to Intercept and Obstruct Terrorism Act of 2001
Q3 2
Q4 2008

Q5 Vladimir Arutyunian
Q6 *41: A Portrait of My Father*
Q7 Salt Lake City, Utah
Q8 Killian documents controversy
Q9 Episcopal Church
Q10 Oil painting

Barack Obama 1 (easy)

Q1 Illinois
Q2 African American
Q3 Michelle
Q4 Joe Biden
Q5 Kenya
Q6 Hussein
Q7 John McCain
Q8 Democratic Party
Q9 Columbia University
Q10 Obamacare

Barack Obama 2 (average)

Q1 Honolulu, Hawaii
Q2 2
Q3 Hillary Clinton
Q4 Russia
Q5 Libya
Q6 Osama bin Laden
Q7 Same sex marriage
Q8 Sandy Hook Elementary School
Q9 Paris Agreement
Q10 Ukraine

Barack Obama 3 (expert)

Q1 2009
Q2 University of Chicago Law School
Q3 2
Q4 Cuba

Q5 2
Q6 Alan Keyes
Q7 Denver, Colorado
Q8 Bo and Sunny
Q9 Chicago White Sox
Q10 Protestantism

Donald Trump 1 (easy)

Q1 3
Q2 John
Q3 Hillary Clinton
Q4 Lyin' Ted
Q5 Cleveland, Ohio
Q6 Mike Pence
Q7 Melania
Q8 None
Q9 New York
Q10 Oldest person to become President

Donald Trump 2 (average)

Q1 Rex Tillerson
Q2 White House Press Secretary
Q3 *Trump: The Art of the Deal*
Q4 *The Apprentice*
Q5 James Comey
Q6 Make America Great Again
Q7 Jerusalem
Q8 Singapore
Q9 Nevada
Q10 Brett Kavanaugh

Donald Trump 3 (expert)

Q1 Travel ban (executive order)
Q2 Trans-Pacific Partnership
Q3 Michael Cohen
Q4 Wharton School of the University of Pennsylvania

Q5 Blenheim Palace

Q6 Jeff Sessions

Q7 John McCain

Q8 House of Representatives (Democratic), Senate (Republican)

Q9 Wall along USA-Mexico border

Q10 Patient Protection and Affordable Care Act (Obamacare)

Also by B.R. Egginton

Non-fiction

Edward VI: England's Boy King

Edward VI's Chronicle (Edward VI)

Richard II: The Tyranny of the White Hart

The Princes in the Tower: An Enigma… 500 Years in the Making

Nicholas II: The Fall of the Romanovs

Henry Hotze: The Master of Confederate Diplomacy

Historiography for Beginners

Archaeology for Beginners

Twelve Olympians: The Greek Pantheon Made Easy

History Essay Writing Basics: For High School and Undergraduate Students

Shorthand SOS: Learn Teeline Shorthand FAST

Public Affairs for Journalists: Concise Edition

Ice Hockey Rulebook

Fiction

The Sixth Number

A Kingdom of Our Own

The Chronicles of Ascension

History Quest: The Plot

The Prince and the Pauper: Annotated Edition (Mark Twain)

Trivia

The Ultimate History Quiz

The Ultimate Mythology Quiz

The Ultimate British Royal Navy Quiz

The Ultimate British Prime Ministers Quiz

The Ultimate English Monarchs Quiz

The Ultimate French Monarchs Quiz

www.ingramcontent.com/pod-product-compliance
Lightning Source LLC
Chambersburg PA
CBHW051344280526
45784CB00007B/2807